THE "POISONED SPRING"

OF ECONOMIC LIBERTARIANISM

Menger, Mises, Hayek, Rothbard:

A critique from Catholic social teaching

of the 'Austrian school' of economics

ANGUS SIBLEY

Paris, France

Published by

PAX ROMANA

CATHOLIC MOVEMENT FOR INTELLECTUAL AND CULTURAL AFFAIRS

USA

in partnership with

CATHOLIC SCHOLARS FOR WORKER JUSTICE

and the

CATHOLIC LABOR NETWORK

VOLUME ONE
IN THE SERIES ON

CATHOLIC SOCIAL TEACHING AND
CONTEMPORARY SOCIAL-ECOLOGICAL THOUGHT

ISBN-13: 978-1461144564
ISBN-10: 1461144566

Printed by CreateSpace
www.createspace.com

PAX ROMANA / CMICA-USA
1025 Connecticut Avenue NW, Suite 1000
Washington DC 20036
pax-romana-cmica-usa@omcast.net
www.pax-romana-cmica-usa.org

ANGUS SIBLEY studied mathematics and economics at Edinburgh University and later qualified as an actuary. Pursuing a career in investment, he became a member of the London Stock Exchange. Now retired, he lives with his wife Aurora in Paris. He has long been concerned by the damaging effects on our economies and societies of the doctrinaire application of free-market theory. He has published many articles on

this subject in newspapers and journals in Britain, America, France and Ireland. In this book he draws upon his professional experience and theological knowledge to show how 'libertarian' economic theory and practice are radically challenged by Catholic teaching. Summarizing his argument, he writes:

Capitalism is like the electric motor traditionally used in subway trains: a very useful machine which has the peculiarity that it must never be allowed to run free when not connected to the wheels of a train. For without the restraint due to the train's inertia, the motor will accelerate wildly till its rotating centre disintegrates. That does not mean that the motor is defective; it simply means that it only works properly under restraint. Likewise, our markets, when allowed to operate without an adequate framework of limitations, tend to run wild; they become financially, economically and socially destructive.

Yet many economists, particularly those of the 'Austrian school', reject this principle. They call for deregulated, unhampered markets under minimal political control. By heeding these theorists, we have got ourselves into deep trouble. It is important that we understand why this ideology, so widely accepted, often subconsciously, is fundamentally flawed and particularly unsuited to the needs of our times.

Catholic Social Teaching offers an alternative approach to economics. It insists upon firm and effective regulation of markets, refuses to regard labor as mere merchandise, and highlights the vital importance of politics in creating a just society.

Many of Angus Sibley's essays on economic and other topics can be found on his personal website:

www.equilibrium-economicum.net

PAX ROMANA / CMICA-USA

www.pax-romana-cmica-usa.org

Pax Romana / Catholic Movement for Intellectual and Cultural Affairs - USA is the US Pax Romana federation for lay Catholic intellectuals and professionals. The worldwide Pax Romana movement, which works closely with the United Nations and the Holy See, has more than 120 years of history and networks some 240,000 intellectuals, professionals, and university students across 80 countries. The mission of the US Pax Romana intellectual-professional federation is to research, study, and promote Catholic Social Teaching for the new World Church and for the new Global Civilization.

CATHOLIC SCHOLARS FOR WORKER JUSTICE

www.catholicscholarsforworkerjustice.org

Catholic Scholars for Worker Justice promotes Catholic Social Teaching on the rights of workers and the indispensible role that unions play in securing justice for workers and their families, in the workplace, for the universal common good. Its purpose is to engage in scholarly research and publication on Catholic Social Teaching as it applies to workers' rights and social responsibilities; to work with all parties to recognize the right of workers to freely join a union of their choosing without fear of reprisal from any party; to insure that workers' rights are respected in union organizing campaigns at all institutions and corporations; and to stand in solidarity with workers on every continent who may be shunned, fired, jailed, tortured, or even killed for the advocacy of social justice and the right to organize.

CATHOLIC LABOR NETWORK

www.catholiclabor.org

The Catholic Labor Network hopes to be a place for those Catholics, lay, religious and clergy, who are active in their churches and in unions, to learn about their Church's teachings as regards labor issues, to pray for those who are working for economic justice, and to share information about events and struggles that may be taking place in their area. For over one hundred years, the Catholic Church has been a voice of support for workers, and a conscience to the body politic when it ponders issues dealing with the distribution of wealth and the condition of workers.

The right ordering of economic life cannot be left to a free competition of forces. For from this source, as from a **poisoned spring**, have originated and spread all the errors of individualist economic teaching. Destroying through forgetfulness or ignorance the social and moral character of economic life, it held that economic life must be considered and treated as altogether free from and independent of public authority, because in the market, i.e., in the free struggle of competitors, it would have a principle of self direction which governs it much more perfectly than would the intervention of any created intellect. But free competition, while justified and certainly useful provided it is kept within certain limits, clearly cannot direct economic life – a truth which the outcome of the application in practice of the tenets of this evil individualistic spirit has more than sufficiently demonstrated. Therefore, it is most necessary that economic life be again subjected to and governed by a true and effective directing principle ... Hence ... it is most necessary ... to establish a juridical and social order which will, as it were, give form and shape to all economic life.

Pope Pius XI

QUADRAGESIMO ANNO

1931 Papal Encyclical, Par. 88, bold emphasis added.
This paragraph is the source of the phrase the "Poisoned Spring"
used in the title of this book.

ACKNOWLEDGMENTS

M y heartfelt thanks are due to Joe Holland, who originally suggested this book, and who has undertaken a great deal of patient work in editing it for publication by Pax Romana; as well as to Fr Sinclair Oubré, founder of the Catholic Labor Network, who introduced Joe Holland to my work, and to the Catholic Labor Network and Catholic Scholars for Social Justice, co-sponsors of the publication. My acknowledgements are due also to the many publishers who have granted permission for the reprint of their copyright material:

- *Biblical citations (save where otherwise mentioned) are excerpts from THE NEW JERUSALEM BIBLE, copyright © 1985 by Darton, Longman & Todd, Ltd, and Doubleday, a division of Random House, Inc. Reprinted by permission.*

- *Citations from Vatican documents, © Libreria Editrice Vaticana, are reprinted with permission.*

- *Acton Institute, for texts by Robert Sirico.*

- *American Enterprise Institute, for texts by Michael Novak.*

- *Columbia University Press, for texts by Thomas Woods.*

- *Lexington Books, for texts by Thomas Woods.*

- *Libertarian Press, Inc., for texts by Carl Menger and Ludwig von Mises.*

- *Ludwig von Mises Institute, for texts by Murray Rothbard.*

- *Rowman & Littlefield (and Madison Books), for texts by Michael Novak.*

- *Taylor & Francis (Routledge) for texts by Friedrich von Hayek, Friedrich von Wieser and John Gray.*

- *University of Chicago Press, for texts by Friedrich von Hayek.*

TABLE OF CONTENTS

PREFACE

JOE HOLLAND, PH.D.

Professor of Philosophy & Religion, St. Thomas University of Miami Gardens, Florida
President, Pax Romana / Catholic Movement for Intellectual and Cultural Affairs USA
Vice-Chairperson, Catholic Scholars for Worker Justice

Libertarianism versus Catholic Social Teaching

F or some time I have been concerned about the appearance of Catholic apologists for libertarian economics, and all the more concerned about Catholic intellectuals who even claim support from Catholic Social Teaching for this dangerous ideological perspective. As a philosopher and theologian who has long been a careful student of the Church's rich tradition of social ethics, I knew that such a claim cannot be upheld. Because of strong philosophical and theological reasons, Catholic Social Teaching represents the very antithesis of libertarianism.

How delighted I was, therefore, when Fr. Sinclair Oubre, founder and Spiritual Moderator of the Catholic Labor Network, shared with me the essays of Angus Sibley, a retired member of the London Stock Exchange and now living in Paris. Angus had been publishing essays on economics through his Internet website, and quite a few of these essays offered insightful criticisms of one

1

of the dominant intellectual sources of libertarian economics, namely the Austrian School. Further, the essays were frequently grounded in Catholic Social Teaching, though also in economic theory and in Angus' own business experience.

After being continually impressed with the essays, I began an email correspondence with Angus and eventually invited him to write this book, which I felt was much needed. It took a great deal of work on his part and he did a splendid job. Regretfully, the book was delayed in being published due to my limited time for editorial assistance amidst an overly busy life. So I am grateful to Angus not only for this brilliant study, but also for his generous patience.

I am also grateful that Pax Romana / Catholic Movement for Intellectual and Cultural Affairs - USA is publishing this important book, and that it is being co-sponsored by two "soul-mate" organizations in the defense of authentic Catholic Social Teaching, namely the Catholic Labor Network and Catholic Scholars for Worker Justice.

Before launching into the text, I would like to add a few reflections of my own on the question of libertarian economics. These reflections will be largely in philosophy, for that is what I teach, but also somewhat in theology, which I also occasionally teach. In both cases, they bear upon the dramatic clash between, and therefore the non-compatibility of, libertarian philosophy and Catholic Social Teaching.

If, however, dear reader, you are not of a philosophical temperament, please do not be put off by the abstract nature of these reflections. Instead, jump over this Preface and go directly to Angus Sibley's more readable and engaging chapters.

Libertarian Philosophy of Individualism

The first and most fundamental clash between the libertarian and Catholic visions is that, while libertarianism sees the human person as an *autonomous individual*, Catholic Social Teaching – on both philosophical and theological grounds – understands the human person as *by nature social*, including in economic life.

The libertarian doctrine of the autonomous individual finds its immediate intellectual roots in the atomistic philosophy of the modern European Enlightenment. For example, when the Austrian School's Friedrich von Hayek (1899-1902) appealed in his writings for justification of libertarianism to "Western Civilization," it was to this modern source that he referred, and not to the classical Western intellectual tradition. The mainstream of Modern Enlightenment philosophy argued that the human person is without natural organic bonds to others.

The modern Enlightenment doctrine of individual autonomy had earlier theological roots in the Protestant Reformation, particularly its Calvinist expression. The Reformation in turn drew on the individualist voluntarism of the Medieval British Franciscan philosopher-theologian William of Ockham. It portrayed Christian conversion and salvation as radically individualistic and voluntarist. But exploring those deeper roots would be too much for this brief Preface.

Enlightenment individualism had more ancient roots in the pre-Socratic Greek philosopher Democritus of Abera (460–370

3

BCE) and the later Greek philosopher Epicurus (341-270 BCE), an Athenian who settled on the Greek island of Samos. We have little writing from Democritus but much from Epicurus, so he is the more famous. Drawing on Democritus, Epicurus taught a doctrine of cosmic materialism, rejected religion, denied life after death, and portrayed all of reality as made up of blindly driven "atoms." He used Greek word *atomos* to define the ultimately smallest "un-cuttable" particles of matter, which he saw as blindly colliding with each other within a great cosmic "void."

The Epicurean philosophy carried over to classical Roman ci-vilization, where the philosopher-poet Lucretius (c.99-c.55 BCE) authored the epic poem *DE RERUM NATURA* (On the Nature of Things). In the European Renaissance, early modern Western scientists (then called "natural philosophers") enthusiastically adopted the Epicurean worldview from Renaissance translations of Lucretius' famous work. Initially, these natural philosophers combined Epicurean materialism in science with a voluntarist Ockhamite or Deist theology, but over time such theological com-panions typically fell to the wayside, leaving only atomist mate-rialism.

The modern Western Enlightenment philosophers then ap-plied modern "scientific" atomism, with its doctrinal roots in De-mocritus, Epicurus, and Lucretius, to a modern atomized "scientif-ic" understanding of human nature and human society. Thus, the birth of the modern "social sciences," including economics.

For the ethics of this voluntarist-materialist cosmology, Epicu-rus had reduced good and evil respectively to sensations of plea-sure and pain. So he and his followers sought withdrawal from politics to privately maximize pleasure (not in gross fashion, but rather in subtle ways) and especially to minimize pain. Much later, in the recent nineteenth century, this same doctrine would become the philosophical foundation of utilitarian ethics, but without the withdrawal from political life.

In the early modern social-scientific paradigm, the human correlative of autonomous, voluntaristic, materialist atoms moving within the cosmic void became autonomous individuals pursuing only their voluntary material "interests" in society. Within that framework, modern "scientific" economics became the study of how humans pursue these "interests" through the material processes of extraction, production, distribution, and consumption.

But the early economists seem to have forgotten about nature's additional dimension of *reproduction*. And so the modern "scientific" paradigm for economics in both free-market capitalist and state-dominated socialist models would ultimately lead in our times to a global crisis of ecological sustainability.

In the autonomous libertarian perspective, economics, politics, and culture get reduced to individual choices of autonomous wills, based on an individual's "interests," which themselves are seen as only arbitrary expressions of will. Further, for libertarianism the only form of social structure becomes voluntary contracts made by such autonomous individuals.

Defenders of this theory, while seeing marriage only as a contract, have never been able to explain how small pre-rational children can make valid familial contracts. Perhaps it is not surprising that so many marriages, when understood only as an "interest" based contract of autonomous individuals, also are proving non-sustainable.

Social Nature of the Human Person

By contrast, Catholic Social Teaching draws on far different philosophical and theological views of the human person.

Philosophically, the Catholic tradition has followed the position of Aristotle that the human person is *naturally social*, and that human society itself is rooted in and constitutes an organic development of the family, although each larger social form beyond family (e.g., the village and later the city-state) has its own distinct social logic. That Greek tradition from Aristotle deepened with the Roman Stoics, who claimed that all humans belong by nature to a single global social-ecological community, which they called "cosmopolis."

This naturally social understanding of the human continued in classical European Catholic legal traditions and later found new strength with the Catholic Medieval Aristotelian renaissance led by Thomas Aquinas. From there it flowed into the seeds of human rights and international law as developed by the early modern Catholic philosophical and theological school of Salamanca in Spain. Ultimately, it found mature modern expression in contemporary Catholic Social Teaching.

Theologically, the Bible is our greatest witness to the social nature of the human person, and to the social responsibilities of the organic human social bond. A dramatically negative expression of this biblical doctrine may be found in the murderer Cain's notorious cry in Genesis 4:9: *Am I my brother's keeper?* A dramatically positive expression may be found in the Lord's decision to liberate the enslaved "children of Israel" (a family metaphor) from their oppression by the rulers of the Egyptian Empire – not as individuals, but as a people. This liberation is announced in Exodus 3:7-8: *I have witnessed the affliction of my people in Egypt ... Therefore, I have come down to rescue them.*

Lastly, the COMPENDIUM OF THE SOCIAL DOCTRINE OF THE CHURCH, the most current authoritative expression of the Catholic social magisterium, clearly confirms this understanding of the human person when it boldly states: *The human person is essentially a social being.*[1]

This, of course, fits in with our everyday experience of family. The human being is born of the biological mixing of the DNA of a mother and father. The parents are in turn genetically indebted to their families of origin, including all prior generations of their families, all the way back to our human family's common evolutionary origin in Africa, and beyond that to all of biological evolution.

So the child enters the world within the micro-society of the family, which is the first source of its social care, and the child is genetically part of a vast ecological network of extended family, which ultimately reaches to the entire human family and even deeper into the ancient roots of the planetary biosphere.

In the extreme and tragic case of an abandoned baby who is not constantly touched in love (in effect, the closest real example to the false image of an "autonomous individual"), we sadly discover the pathological situation of the "non-bonded child." In such cases,

---

[1] Pontifical Council for Justice and Peace, COMPENDIUM OF THE SOCIAL DOCTRINE OF THE CHURCH (Cittá del Vaticano : Libreria Editrice Vaticana, 2004), Par. 149.

unless there is extensive therapeutic intervention, the child will fail to develop an ethical conscience and typically, albeit tragically, such a child will grow up to a life of crime.

So, since we are by nature social, the libertarian philosophy is grounded on a fundamental philosophical error about the very nature of the human person, and a dangerous one at that. The words of Austrian economist Friedrich von Hayek express this error in striking and memorable form: he claims that, in the free market, we rightly and properly *gain from **not** treating one another as neighbors.*[2]

Individualism in Utilitarian Ethics

We can see how dangerous this error becomes when we explore this philosophically materialist idea of an autonomous individual in its modern correlative form of philosophical ethics, namely *utilitarianism*. Utilitarian ethics is not normally thought of as libertarian because of its altruistic orientation, but it is nonetheless rooted in and still manifests the same philosophical error.

Society is claimed by utilitarians to be nothing more than a collection of autonomous individuals making voluntaristic individual choices, with social bonds being only those of voluntarily chosen contracts. This school of philosophical ethics accepts the Epicurean doctrine that good and evil are reducible to feelings of pleasure and pain. But utilitarianism seeks – legally or ethically – to direct those choices in a magnanimous direction.

Jeremy Bentham (1748-1832) and John Stuart Mill (1806-1873), the sequential creators of modern utilitarian ethics, pointed Epicu-

---

[2] Friedrich von Hayek, THE FATAL CONCEIT (London: Routledge, 1988), p. 13.

reanism toward altruistic legal reforms for society. Bentham initially sought to calculate mathematically whatever would bring the greatest pleasure and least pain to the largest number of individuals, and to guide reforming legislation by this principle. Mill later added a hierarchy of higher and lower pleasures, with the former receiving more weight.

In the utilitarian view, the individual's psychological experiences of pleasure and pain become neurological guides for the autonomous individual's volitional "interests," with their social expression found in individual electoral choices and market choices. In a return to the Epicurean withdrawal from politics, some contemporary economic libertarians have argued that market choices are the truly fundamental ones, more so than political choices, as in "one dollar, one vote."

Utilitarian ethics, because of its underlying materialist philosophy, must ultimately reject any other ethical norms beyond pleasure and pain. In such a reductionist philosophical approach, ethics must of necessity become relativistic (determined only by majority choices), and any ethical criteria beyond a quantitative calculus of individuals' pleasure and pain must be rejected.

A fundamental problem with such a view is that humans are not the only animals who experience pleasure and pain. So, ultimately, despite efforts to the contrary, utilitarianism's underlying philosophy of atomistic individualism must logically lead to an undermining of the doctrine of universal human rights. Even the United Nations Universal Declaration of Human Rights, which is not grounded in such a utilitarian calculus, must eventually yield to this reductionist and relativist ethics.

Thus, Peter Singer (born 1946), probably the world's leading utilitarian philosopher, has argued that any notion of a special universal "dignity of human life" is simply nonsense, and so he has called for the killing of handicapped children. Praising what he calls *selective medical infanticide*, Singer writes – apparently with approval – that *killing unwanted infants ... has been a normal practice in most societies throughout human history.*[3]

Might such an anti-human practice, and other related rejections of human rights, be on the future horizon of a libertarian society?

Negative Social Contract State
Versus Positive Common Good State

These theories of autonomous individuals and utilitarian ethics also ground the libertarian understanding of politics. Pursuing their own individual interests, individuals are seen by libertarians as making human relationships only through the form of contracts among autonomous individuals, be it the business contract, the contract of marriage, or the social contract of the state.

Reducing the foundation of the state to merely a social contract, libertarians see government as an artificial institution created voluntaristically by autonomous individuals.

Further, the Reformation background of earlier libertarian theorists, particularly Calvinism, had seen the state as necessary only because of original sin. Theologically, this was a step backwards from Thomas Aquinas to Augustine, reflecting the view of many Reformers that medieval theology was a misguided diver-

---

[3] Peter Singer, RETHINKING LIFE AND DEATH: THE COLLAPSE OF OUR TRADITIONAL ETHICS (New York: St. Martin's Press, 1994), pp. 1-4 & 128-131.

sion from earlier, and in their view more authentic, Christian theologies like that of Augustine.

Without sin, it was claimed, there would be no need for the state, so the state was created to restrain the evils flowing from original sin. Obviously, such a state could not positively pursue the common good because as a post-fall institution the state was designed by God only to restrain sinful evil. Should it seek something more, it would become blasphemous and idolatrous.

While libertarianism wishes to minimize government and to restrict it mainly to the negative function of protecting individuals from harm, Catholic Social Teaching – again, on both philosophical and theological grounds – certainly understands government as having this negative role of restraining evil, but also as positively charged with pursing common good of all its citizens.

Catholic Social Teaching, like Aristotle, sees the state as a natural social institution primarily directed to promoting the common good. For Catholic theology, even had there been no original sin, the state would still be necessary and government's role basically positive.

For it sees all expressions of humanity's social nature – at every level from the family to the state, and from the local to the global – as requiring the principle of governance, which (when just) is seen as human participation in the divine governance of the cosmos.

This is why today, when we experience late modern "globalization" of economic markets, Catholic Social Teaching strongly insists on the political need for both international law and global governance of the "family of nations," including economic governance. In that regard, the Holy See ("Vatican"), following Catholic Social Teaching, provides constant support for the United Nations, even while calling for its improvement through institutional reform.

Of course, there can be great problems with governments at every level, but the authentic Catholic response to such problems is fundamentally different from the libertarian one. While libertarians instinctively call for minimizing government, and some even for eliminating it, Catholic Social Teaching calls for reforming government.

For the Catholic tradition, the answer to bad government is not eliminating its positive functions but improving them. Its alternative to bad government is not less or no government, but good or better government.

For, again, Catholic Social Teaching sees the most basic purpose of government as promoting and serving the common good of all.

Similarly, in the sterile debate over whether the state or the market should lead, the Catholic argument is neither for one nor the other, but rather for cooperation between the two.

Again, in this cooperation the primary positive role of government is to ensure the common good, including the economic common good, which it argues cannot be achieved by the market alone.

Conversely, it argues that the common good cannot be achieved by the state alone, since the state's function is to ensure order and justice in the market, not to replace the market.

Contentious Issues:
Property, Unions, and Subsidiarity

We also see a great difference between the Catholic and libertarian positions in the question of *property* and, in a related manner, in the question of *labor unions*, both of which are related to the important principle of *subsidiarity*.

Property

In the libertarian tradition, the ownership of "private" property is seen as the primary "interest" which the state is called upon to defend for supposedly autonomous property-owning individuals. Indeed, for many libertarians the principle of private property seems to be a moral absolute, a matter of individual interest that often seems inextricably linked to the very identity of the autonomous self.

Thus, the late American libertarian philosopher Robert Nozick (1938–2002) argued that every individual has an absolute right to whatever assets he or she acquires lawfully. So, if the state imposes extra taxes on very rich persons, it infringes those persons' fundamental rights.[4] Likewise, the late American libertarian economist Milton Friedman (1912-2006) asserted that *there is a fundamental conflict between the ideal of 'fair shares' and the ideal of personal liberty.*[5]

In the Catholic tradition, by contrast, property is not completely "private," though the tradition does support individual property as a valuable social development.

---

[4] Nozick, ANARCHY, STATE AND UTOPIA (New York: Basic Books, 1974), chap. 7, *passim.*
[5] Milton & Rose Friedman, FREE TO CHOOSE (San Diego: Harcourt, 1980), chap. 5.

For Catholic Social Teaching, the fundamental principle here is "the universal destination of goods," which means that the Creator, who is the "owner" of all creation, has destined the goods of creation for all.[6] In so far as individual property serves this principle (which is a variant of the principle of the common good), then individual property is legitimate.

But when individual property becomes too concentrated in a small minority in a manner that does not serve the common good, then individual property can become illegitimate, and the state would need to support better use of property for the common good. Another way of expressing this principle has been to say that private property carries a social mortgage. Explaining this social mortgage and its root in the universal destination of goods, the COMPENDIUM highlights the Catholic principle of the "preferential option for the poor."

> *The principle of the universal destination of goods requires that the poor, the marginalized and in all cases those whose living conditions interfere with their proper growth should be the focus of particular concern. To this end, the preferential option for the poor should be reaffirmed in all its force.[7]*

Further, because libertarians are frequently hostile to the ecological movement, we need to recall that the "universal destination of goods" also means that the goods of creation are given by the Creator for the ecological well being of all of creation, and not just for the human "utility" of consumerism. Again, we turn to the COMPENDIUM which criticizes the entire modern era as having a

---

[6] COMPENDIUM, Pars. 171 ff.
[7] COMPENDIUM, Par. 182

reductionist, mechanistic, and utilitarian attitude that leads to undermining the integrity of the natural world:

> *The tendency toward an "ill-considered" exploitation of the resources of creation is the result of a long historical and cultural process. The modern era ... has even reached the point of threatening the environment's hospitable aspect: the environment as 'resource' risks threatening the environment as 'home' ... This reductionist conception views the natural world in mechanistic terms and sees development in terms of consumerism ... A correct understanding of the environment prevents the utilitarian reduction of nature to a mere object to be manipulated and exploited.*[8]

We may compare this with the attitude of Carl Menger (1840-1921), founder of the Austrian School of economics. He condemned restraints on competition on the ground that such restraints prevent production and consumption from reaching maximum levels.

Unions

In a similar manner, libertarians are generally hostile to labor unions. At best, they typically reduce the issue to one of individual choice. But in Catholic Social Teaching, unions represent what are called "mediating institutions." As such, they are not reducible simply to matters of personal choice but stand as social institutions indispensible for the common good of industrial societies. Their absence would leave workers at the mercy of concentrated corporate power or concentrated state power, or still worse a combination of the two.

---

[8] COMPENDIUM, Pars. 461-463.

We could say then that unions as mediating institutions represent the principle of subsidiarity in the economic sphere. Just as in the political sphere subsidiarity defends the principle of the *priority of the family* against unjust intrusions by the state, so here in the economic sphere subsidiarity defends what Catholic Social Teaching calls the principle of *an intrinsic priority of labor over capital.*[9]

For this reason, the COMPENDIUM defends workers' *right to assemble and form associations,* and it describes unions both as *an indispensible element of social life* and as *promoters of the struggle for social justice.*[10] Further, in the light of *ever more rapid processes of economic and financial globalization,* the COMPENDIUM calls for *unions to engage in renewal ... to act in new ways ... pursuing 'new forms of solidarity' ...* [that entail] *greater responsibilities.*[11] Lastly, never seeing labor and capital as philosophical enemies, it praises *the [cooperative] relationship between labor and capital [found] when workers participate in ownership, management, and profits.*[12]

Nonetheless, there are situations where unions can become evil, just as families can become evil, just as businesses can become evil, and just as governments can become evil. But the truly Catholic response is not to reject the principle of unionism, any more than to reject the principle of family, or of business, or of government. Rather, the truly Catholic response would be to seek reform of the institution, that is, to attempt to transform bad unionism into good unionism.

---

[9] Ibid., Pars. 214 & 277.
[10] Ibid., Par. 301, 305, & 306.
[11] Ibid., Par. 309.
[12] Ibid., Par. 281.

Subsidiarity

Finally, some Catholic libertarians appeal to Catholic Social Teaching's principle of "subsidiarity" as an argument against government. The principle of subsidiarity, which in Catholic Social Teaching is usually applied to politics, means that nothing should be done at a higher level that could be done at a lower level. It also means that it is the function of the higher level – the state in the political arena – to help, that is to "subsidize," the lower level to handle the function in question.[13]

One example of a libertarian misunderstanding of this principle argues that the government should not provide social insurance for care of the needy elderly, but should leave it to their families. Yet subsidiarity does not mean that the government should abandon financial support for such care, but rather that the state should financially help (subsidize) families themselves to care for their needy elderly; the state should not treat the latter simply as autonomous individuals, condemned to "stand on their own feet" even when they cannot.

I might suggest here that such "pro-family" aid would in many cases probably be well directed to home-care by relatives, which could normally prove less expensive than the cost of nursing homes, be they owned by government or by business corporations. Of course, nursing homes would still be necessary, for there would certainly be needy elderly persons whose care is beyond the ability of a typical family or who no longer have family members

---

[13] Ibid., Pars. 185-188.

to care for them. In such cases, the principle of subsidiarity would not apply, and the state should quite legitimately ensure their care.

Conclusion

After signaling the stark contrast between libertarianism and Catholic Social Teaching, let us now turn to the splendid text of Angus Sibley's book. In doing so, let us also thank him for such profound research and for such thoughtful insights. Through this book, he has done a great service to the rich tradition of Catholic Social Teaching, and to the human family which it humbly serves.

RETURN TO ECONOMIC LIBERTARIANISM

The problem is to live with the market without being devoured by it.
The present crisis shows us how and why we are devoured by the
market: we have, as it were, allowed our horses to bolt.
ROBERT CASTEL [1]

CLASSICAL FREE-MARKET DOCTRINE

The doctrine of the untrammeled free market, or *economic libertarianism*, is an idea which has its roots in the age of the European Enlightenment. The belief that all human beings are born free and equal is taken to imply that any person is morally, and should be legally, entitled to enter freely into any contract with any other person by mutual agreement.[2] This is the kernel of the doctrine of *laissez-faire*.

The market is an arena of interaction of contracting parties. The parties (market participants) are essentially all of us: buyers and sellers, employers and employees, investors and borrowers. If there are restrictions on the freedom of market participants to con-

---

[1] Robert Castel, "Psychanalyse de la crise," LE MONDE (Paris), 27 February 2009. The writer is a sociologist.
[2] This refers to persons other than minors or others lacking capacity.

tract howsoever they wish with each other, then we do not have a fully free market.

In practice, interference comes from two sources. An external authority may regulate the market by ruling that certain contracts, or certain contract terms, are not permissible. Thus, US federal minimum wage laws prohibit contracts of employment where the rate of pay is (as from July 2009) less than $7.25 per hour. Alternatively, market participants may agree among themselves to restrict their own freedom of contract. Thus, a labor union may restrain its members from contracting to work more than, say, 45 hours per week.

Objections to Market Restraints

According to libertarian economists, all such restrictions should be avoided, for three main reasons.

- *Personal Liberty.* First, they claim that any interference with freedom of contract is an unacceptable intrusion upon personal liberty.

- *Economic Efficiency.* Second, they believe that the fully free market is the most economically efficient system. This means that it is conducive to the highest possible levels of production and consumption of goods and services, or *greatest consumer benefit*, as economists put it.

- *Market Knows Best.* Third, they argue that interference with the market is often practiced with a view to realizing some particular vision of the kind of society that we (or an influential proportion of us) desire. Libertarians hold that any such objective is fundamentally objectionable.

Primarily, because they see it as prejudicial to personal freedom; for libertarians any attempt by society to pursue a desired common goal is redolent of fascism or communism. And also because they believe that nobody – no private individual, no political leader, no governing body of any kind – can know what is best for the community. Only the market – as the synthesis of the desires of the individuals who make up the community – can know what is best.

They deny in principle that there is any 'common good' other than the sum of individual goods, the aggregate of personal individual satisfactions. Supporters of free market doctrine thus justify it on both moral and practical grounds. It is a libertarian, materialistic and highly individualistic doctrine.

Justifications for Market Restraints

My argument is that there are serious objections to this doctrine on all three points mentioned above.

- *The Strong over the Weak.* It is argued that any contract mutually agreed between two (or more) parties is *ipso facto* acceptable; and, since one should not be hindered from doing what is acceptable, therefore any restriction of freedom of contract is an unjustifiable intrusion upon the freedom of the contracting parties. But the major premise of this syllogism is false. In reality, contracting parties are frequently of unequal strength. For example, a mutually agreed contract between a poor laborer and a rich employer may be inequitable in favor of the stronger party, therefore morally unacceptable.

21

- *Ecological Inefficiency.* It is also argued that the fully free market is the most efficient way to maximize production and consumption. But one of our key problems today is overconsumption by human beings of natural resources. It follows that the free market is the best way of achieving an unacceptable goal.

- *Fallacy of Composition.* Lastly, it is argued that there is no common good other than the sum of personal goods. This argument falls foul of the fallacy of composition. For example, during a recession, individuals see it as conducive to their own personal good to spend as little as possible, to put aside savings against future trouble. But this behavior by individuals reduces overall demand and aggravates the recession. The sum of personal goods conflicts with the common good.

The city of Paris as it developed in the nineteenth century, essentially as we know it today, was built under very strict planning controls. These were seen by many at the time as irksome, authoritarian restrictions on the freedom of property owners to build as they wished. Yet under those rules was built one of the most beautiful cities in the world. That is not merely my personal view as a Parisian. Of all the world's cities, Paris is one of the most visited and admired, one of the most celebrated in art and literature. It is a resplendent argument against the libertarian rejection of central planning.

CHALLENGES TO LAISSEZ-FAIRE

Since economic science as we know it began with the 'classical' economists of the eighteenth century, we have seen a continuing dialectic between the libertarian economic philosophy and its antagonist, the belief that *the market should be appropriately controlled*, as Pope John Paul II put it.[3]

Marxist and Christian Challenges

The classical free-market paradigm was dominant from the late eighteenth century until well into the nineteenth, but its failings led to grave social problems and the rise of intellectual challenges to the free-market view. The best-known challenge was of course Marxism, which burst into the open with the COMMUNIST MANIFESTO of 1848.

But many other anti-free-market schools of thought were developing. In the religious world, Catholic leaders such as Jean-Baptiste Henri Lacordaire in France, Wilhelm Emmanuel von Ketteler in Germany, and John A. Ryan in America denounced the abuses of *laissez-faire*; there were similar reactions in Protestant churches and in reformist political movements.

German Historical School

In the world of academic economics, the main challenge developed in Germany with the *Historical School* of economists, so called because their analysis was founded on studies of economic history. They believed that the science of economics should be based on observation of what actually happens in real-life economies, rather than on the theoretical models of economic activity favored by the Classical School.

---

[3] Pope John Paul II, encyclical CENTESIMUS ANNUS (1991), Par. 35.

The Historicists were pragmatic. They were far from being purist free-marketeers; they favored considerable public intervention, central and local, to counteract the socially damaging effects of unrestrained capitalism. From its beginnings in the mid- nineteenth century, the Historical School developed very strongly; it became dominant in Germany and remained so for many decades.

American Institutionalists

Towards the end of the century, a number of American economists studied at German universities and brought the Historical doctrine across the Atlantic. They became known in America as the *Institutionalists*. Here is one of them, Richard T. Ely (both a leading figure in the Protestant Social Gospel movement and one of the founders of the American Economics Association), writing in 1884:

> *In 1876 at the centennial of The Wealth of Nations were brought together representatives of two schools: the older [Classical] school, proud of the age and respectability of their doctrine, but disheartened at the loss of public confidence; the younger [Historical] school, hopeful because convinced that the future belonged to them.*[4]

AUSTRIAN SCHOOL'S COUNTER-CHALLENGE

Meanwhile, in Austria, libertarian academic economists were aghast at this challenge to their beloved classical theory. They decided to fight back, and this gave rise to a long intellectual battle

---

[4] Richard T. Ely, "The Past and Present of Political Economy," JOHNS HOPKINS UNIVERSITY STUDIES IN HISTORY AND POLITICAL SCIENCE (Baltimore: Murray, 1884), Series 2, Part 3, 6.

between Austrian and German academics, known as *der Methoden-streit*, the quarrel over methods.

Ludwig von Mises and Friedrich von Hayek

The later Austrian economists, of whom the best known are Ludwig von Mises and Friedrich von Hayek, became extremely virulent supporters of the free-market principle, since they saw it as a bulwark against totalitarianisms such as they observed in Germany and Russia. They apparently failed to recognize that communism developed as a reaction against the nasty consequences of early nineteenth-century laissez-faire economics.

The German Historicists were themselves very conscious of the communist threat; they saw a benevolent state-regulated capitalist economy as the best defense against it. But Austrians blamed the Historicists for encouraging a statist economy which, they alleged, facilitated the rise of Nazism.

Their Present-Day Followers

Today, followers of Mises and Hayek continue vociferously to proclaim this kind of argument. They want us to believe that any country which embraces a mixed rather than wholly free-market economy is on *the road to serfdom* as Hayek put it; heading straight for totalitarianism.[5] This argument is unconvincing. Most western European states have long pursued mixed-economy strategies while continuing to function in a democratic manner.

---

[5] Friedrich von Hayek, THE ROAD TO SERFDOM (London: Routledge & Kegan Paul, 1944).

During the worldwide preference for more or less state-regulated economies, through and beyond the first half of the last century, Austrian economics had languished in disfavor for nearly a hundred years. But paradoxically, from around 1970 onwards, these economists who were inspired by hatred of communism gained a big worldwide following, just as communism was approaching its own demise.

It seems that the Austrian School's recent popularity largely reflects the great upsurge of individualism that began in the 1960s. For a prime principle of the Austrians is that *the individual takes absolute precedence over the community*.

FAILURE OF
ECONOMIC LIBERTARIANISM

We have now experienced three to four decades of the practical application of this individualist, libertarian, and deregulatory economic philosophy. Its friends justify it by claiming that it has brought increased freedom and prosperity; and so it has, but mainly for a limited number of entrepreneurs, executives and investors. It has also brought us exorbitant inequalities, degradation of employment in quantity and in quality, increasing stresses at work, deterioration in our public amenities, and grave financial instability – to the point where the American banking system has imploded in a disastrous crash, causing severe worldwide damage.

Communist countries carried out a drastic but misguided economic experiment, which ultimately failed. But they had the excuse that it had not been tried before; its miserable outcome was not therefore foreseeable in advance. We have not had this excuse.

We have imposed upon ourselves an experiment which, in essence, has been tried before, in the first half of the nineteenth century, when its consequences were so objectionable that they provoked the rise of the extreme alternative of Marxism.

We have allowed the market to become our tyrannical master rather than our good servant. The time has come to abandon this perverse experiment.

2

DISEASE OF
EXCESSIVE INDIVIDUALISM

Hell consists in man's being unwilling to receive anything,
in his desire to be self-sufficient ... to stand entirely on his own feet...
Hell is wanting-only-to-be-oneself.
POPE BENEDICT XVI [1]

Individualism is a recently-coined expression to which a novel idea
has given birth. Our fathers were only acquainted with égoisme.
ALEXIS DE TOCQUEVILLE [2]

It is impossible to create a good society without ...
some consensus about the kind of society we wish to create.
JONATHAN SACKS [3]

B ehind the plethora of perverse theories and bad practices
from which our economies and societies suffer today, we
perceive an underlying philosophy which we can describe as *exces-*
sive individualism. Legitimate individualism – our quest for the
flourishing of each individual, our support for the rights of the

---

[1] Pope Benedict XVI, INTRODUCTION TO CHRISTIANITY [*Einführung in das Christentum, 1968*], trans. J. R. Foster (San Francisco: Ignatius Press, 1990), 239.
[2] Tocqueville, DEMOCRACY IN AMERICA [*La Démocratie en Amérique, 1835*], trans. Henry Reeve (New York: Knopf, 1945), Vol. II, 98.
[3] Jonathan Sacks, THE POLITICS OF HOPE (London: Vintage [Random House], 2000), 3. The author is Chief Rabbi of the United Kingdom.

individual – is a quintessential and valuable element of modern Western civilization.

It is, however, a double-edged quality which can easily become dangerous by degenerating into egotism, or even anarchism. Therefore, I direct my criticisms not against individualism *per se*, but against its excesses.

EXCESSIVE INDIVIDUALISM
DEFINED

First, two definitions: one by the nineteenth-century French political and social scientist Alexis de Tocqueville, the other by Msgr. John A. Ryan, a twentieth-century American Catholic economist and theologian who was a famous exponent of 'Social Catholicism'. But what these theorists criticize as "individualism" actually represents in my view "excessive individualism;" so please understand the significance of their quotes here as having the latter meaning.

Alexis de Tocqueville's Definition

According to Tocqueville, "individualism" is:

> ... *a mature and calm feeling which disposes each member of the community to sever himself from the mass of his fellows ... so that ... he willingly leaves society at large to itself.*[4]

Tocqueville is severely critical of "individualism," as he defines it:

> *At first it saps only the virtues of public life; but in the long run it attacks and destroys all others, and is at length absorbed in downright selfishness.*[5]

---

[4] Tocqueville, DEMOCRACY IN AMERICA, Vol. II, 98.

He saw it as an evil which could lead to the degradation of the social and political order. For the exaggerated pursuit of personal independence could undermine democratic participation in the governance of society. His argument is reminiscent of Aristotle's concept of the free citizen, one of whose characteristics, and duties, was to take his share in the government of his city:

> *One principle of liberty is for all to rule and be ruled in turn …*
> *this, then, is one note of liberty which all democrats affirm to be*
> *the principle of their state.*[6]

Msgr. John A. Ryan's Definition

According to Ryan, "individualism" is

> *… the tendency to magnify individual liberty, as against exter-*
> *nal authority, and individual activity, as against associated ac-*
> *tivity … through all forms of individualism runs the note of*
> *emphasis upon the importance of self in opposition to either re-*
> *straint or assistance from without.*[7]

Ryan too denounces the consequences. He observes that, according to individualists,

> *… the individual conscience … is not merely the decisive sub-*
> *jective rule, but it is the only rule; there is no objective authority*
> *or standard which it is bound to take into account.*[8]

In other words, one falls into relativism or moral subjectivism. Ryan also complains that "individualists" demand a quasi-

---

[5] Ibid.

[6] Aristotle, POLITICS, tr. Benjamin Jowett (London: Colonial Press, 1900), Book VI, 152 (1317b).

[7] John A. Ryan, "Individualism," THE CATHOLIC ENCYCLOPEDIA, Vol. VII (New York: Appleton, 1910), 761.

[8] Ibid.

anarchic economy of *laissez-faire*, rejecting the regulatory role of the State or of trade unions or trade or professional associations.

EMERGENCE OF
MODERN INDIVIDUALISM

The Protestant Reformation

Modern individualism dates back to the Protestant Reformation which, in the sixteenth century, celebrated the autonomy of the individual Christian as against the tradition and authority of the Catholic Church. Extreme forms of religious individualism made their appearance in certain branches of Protestantism, for example, with the English *Independents* or *Sectaries* of the seventeenth century. They held that any individual was entitled, even without any training or authorization, to set oneself up as a preacher and as head of a church, and thus to disseminate whatsoever doctrine one thought fit.

> *The Sectaries … entertained, as may be supposed, very wild doctrines. Men of an enthusiastic spirit, and sometimes a crazed imagination, as opinionative as they were ignorant, and many of them as ignorant as the lowest vulgar, broached an endless variety of heresies.* [9]

The Enlightenment and America

The eighteenth century, the Age of Enlightenment, was more concerned with the individual's moral and political rights, with the equality of individuals before the law. In the young American re-

---

[9] Sir Walter Scott, TALES OF A GRANDFATHER (1828) (Glasgow: Gowans & Gray, 1928), Second Series, 152.

public, the ideal of *self-reliance* took root and grew vigorously. To-day, in America, this dream is fundamental, forming part of the national tradition. It dates back to the age of the pioneers on the Western frontiers, often little interested in building communities, more concerned to take advantage of the wide open spaces to set themselves up as isolated, independent colonists - as miners or hunters, farmers or cattle-breeders. For them, the cardinal virtue was the capacity and willingness of the individual to live by his own initiative, without the support or direction of others.

This philosophy is doubtless healthy in moderation, but it is perverse and arrogant to push it to extremes. One risks forgetting that, in reality, no one can be entirely self-sufficient; as Fr. Michael O'Halloran SJ, in a sermon at Farm Street Church, London, observed a few years ago, *We are all God's pensioners.* Or, as his colleague Fr. Vincent Hawe SJ remarked on another occasion, *We're not meant to go it alone!*

The French Revolution

Based on the principle that human beings should be equal before the law, the French Revolution promoted the idea that each of us is free, and entitled, to enter into whatever contract he or she wishes with anyone else. A modern French textbook on labor law explains: *laws inspired by the Revolution enshrined the supremacy of the contract, which appeared to be necessarily "fair", between free and equal men.*[10]

---

[10] Brigitte Hess-Fallon & Anne-Marie Simon, DROIT DU TRAVAIL (Paris: Dalloz, 2006), 17.

33

No need, therefore, for, associations of craftsmen or laborers to collectively negotiate terms and conditions of employment. It should be up to each individual to agree to his own contract with his employer. But, in practice, the parties to such a contract are generally of unequal strength. Thus the French Revolution, which was supposed to improve the well-being of the people, led to new legislation which degraded the condition of the workers.

Laws against Workers' Associations

From 1791 till its abrogation in two stages (1864 and 1884), the French *Loi Le Chapelier* prohibited associations (guilds or unions) of tradesmen and other workers. As the authors of the aforesaid textbook observe, *the absence of regulation brought misery for employees, who could not unite to defend their interests.*[11]

The promoter of this law, Isaac Le Chapelier, was a revolutionary Breton advocate famous for his fiery speeches in which he condemned the privileges of the aristocracy and clergy under the *ancien régime.*

In England, similar laws, called the *Combination Acts,* were enacted in 1799 and 1800 in an attempt to suppress *combinations* (associations of industrial workers or craftsmen).

The 1799 Act was backed by William Wilberforce, a Member of Parliament renowned for his campaign against slavery. Another example of the damage done by certain enlightened social reformers to the interests of working people.

---

[11] Ibid.

Semi-Anarchism of the Romantic Age

During the first half of the nineteenth century, individualism veered towards a kind of semi-anarchism, a tendency to reject society's rules, customs and obligations.

This could be emotionally attractive. In songs and operas of haunting beauty, poets and musicians celebrated the triumph of romantic love over social convention. In Kobbé's famous OPERA BOOK we read:

> *It has been suggested – reasonably, I think – that the impossibly violent loves of the romantics were less erotic in origin than manifestations of rebellion against the norms of society.*[12]

But expressions of individualist sentiment could also be negative, virulent, even blasphemous. Thus, Ralph Waldo Emerson wrote that *society everywhere is in conspiracy against the manhood of every one of its members*[13] and that *nothing is at last sacred but the integrity of your own mind.*[14]

For him, society, its traditions and institutions, were simply obstacles to the free development, the spontaneous thought and action, of the individual.

It follows that the individual should be, so far as possible, autonomous and self-reliant. No question, then, of providing any assistance for the individual in difficulty, except within the narrow circle of his immediate family and close friends. *Do not tell me, as a*

---

[12] George Lascelles, Earl of Harewood, KOBBÉ'S COMPLETE OPERA BOOK (London: The Bodley Head, 1987), 393. He is writing about the romantic operas of Vincenzo Bellini (1801–1835).
[13] Ralph Waldo Emerson, essay "Self-Reliance" (1841), EMERSON: ESSAYS AND LECTURES, ed. J. Porte (New York: Literary Classics of the United States, 1983), 261.
[14] Ibid.

good man did the other day, of my obligation to put all poor men in good situations, thundered Emerson in the same essay, adding that, when he was occasionally weak enough to toss the odd dime to a beggar, he felt ashamed of doing so. [15]

Henry David Thoreau, who lived alone for two years in the Walden woods, was another famous despiser of society:

> *Wherever a man goes, men will pursue him and paw him with their dirty institutions, and, if they can, constrain him to belong to their desperate oddfellow society.* [16]

Walt Whitman went so far as to elevate the self to the level of God: *nothing, not God, is greater to one than one's self is.* [17]

ANTI-INDIVIDUALIST REACTION

In the latter decades of the nineteenth century, individualist thought in the West drifted into outright anarchism and lost much popular support.

For the social consequences of jungle capitalism, the product of excessive individualism, brought strong reactions against this philosophy. Trade unionism and socialism developed in Europe, even in America.

---

[15] Ibid., 262.

[16] Henry David Thoreau, WALDEN (1854), THOREAU: A WEEK ON CONCORD, ETC., ed. R. F. Sayre (New York: Literary Classics of the United States, 1985), 459. The word *oddfellow* comes from the name of a kind of mutual benevolent association (*friendly society*) which originated in England in the 18th century and later spread to America and elsewhere. *Oddfellows* met in lodges somewhat like those of Freemasons. Their societies were so named because they contained men of various trades, unlike guilds and early trade unions, which were generally restricted each to one trade. 'Orders of Oddfellows' still exist in many countries.

[17] Walt Whitman, "Song of Myself", no. 48 in LEAVES OF GRASS (1855), WALT WHITMAN: COMPLETE POETRY AND COLLECTED PROSE, ed. J. Kaplan (New York: Literary Classics of the United States, 1982), 84.

Catholic Social Doctrine

Catholic social doctrine, adapted to the sordid realities of industrial society, took shape in the hands of leaders such as Bishop Wilhelm von Ketteler in Germany, the Dominican Henri Lacordaire in France and Cardinal Henry Manning in England, culminating in Pope Leo XIII's encyclical RERUM NOVARUM of 1891. At the dawn of the twentieth century, Msgr. Ryan felt able to state that

> *at present the general trend of ethical theory is away from all forms of individualism, and toward some conception of social welfare as the highest standard.*[18]

Concerning the libertarian theory, which held that social questions such as education, health, morality, and industrial regulation were outside the State's province, Ryan announced triumphantly:

> *This theory has a much smaller following now than it had a century or even half a century ago; for experience has abundantly shown that the assumptions upon which it rests are purely artificial and thoroughly false.*[19]

Strong words indeed from the man known as the "Very Reverend New Dealer," because of his close links with President Franklin Roosevelt.

Tragically, the rejection of excessive individualism fell, in turn, into its own excesses. Among the many anti-individualist movements of the early twentieth century were Bolshevism, fascism and Nazism. These extremisms were intolerable. In reaction, as early as the 1920s, intellectual denunciation of statist philosophies began.

---

[18] Ryan, "Individualism," 762.
[19] Ibid.

INDIVIDUALIST COUNTER-REACTION

Austrian economists Ludwig von Mises and his pupil Friedrich von Hayek began to revile communism, fascism, Nazism; and even moderate socialism, which they saw as a step along the primrose path to collectivist hell. They were largely ignored until the nineteen-sixties.

Then, just as the remaining statisms of the Right were fading away, and as communism was approaching its collapse, the Austrian libertarians attracted attention. And their influence was soon to become overwhelming.

Contempt for Solidarity

Excessive individualist morality insists that each person must live by his own efforts and avoid dependence upon others. It takes a dim view of the notions of solidarity and interdependence. If a rich and successful individualist feels disposed to share some of his affluence with the poor, so be it; but there is no question of recognizing the Jewish and Christian doctrine of a moral or even legal obligation to share.

Tolerance of Inequality

Thus, excessive individualism rejects in principle tax-based redistribution and the welfare state. In practice, this attitude leads to huge inequalities. It is futile to say that, in theory, we are all born equal. Quite apart from any inherited differences in social and financial status, or from accidental misfortunes, the innate differences between personalities are quite sufficient to produce very large differences in personal situations.

There are those who are born rich and die poor, and *vice versa.* There are savers and spendthrifts, money-makers and chronic losers, the clever and the stupid, the robust and the sickly, the hardworking and the lazy, the ambitious and the modest, the greedy and the unworldly.

Excessive individualist doctrine insists that we must accept the consequences of all these differences, which can mean glaring inequalities and a fractured society, with the richest living in fortresses of security, fearful of attacks by the penniless.

The consequence of such attitudes is the reappearance of impoverished, disadvantaged, hopeless underclasses. In the past, these underclasses were often subdued and quiet; today, people are not so easily contented. Those who feel underprivileged are inclined to revolt, as we see in the unhappy suburbs of Paris. Exorbitant inequalities can lead to the breakdown of social order:

> *A society with a substantial propertyless underclass cannot reasonably be expected to be stable when the resentments of those with nothing are open to exploitation by radical movements.* [20]

But extreme individualists detest stability. Hear Emerson again: *People wish to be settled; only so far as they are unsettled is there any hope for them.* [21]

No Limits on Competition

The excessive individualist principle is hostile to any limitation of competition between individuals or, by extension, between their businesses. To restrain competition would interfere with the

---

[20] John Gray, BEYOND THE NEW RIGHT (London: Routledge, 1993), 13. Gray, an English economist and philosopher, is a professor at the London School of Economics.
[21] Ralph Waldo Emerson, "Circles" (1841), EMERSON: ESSAYS AND LECTURES, 413.

commercial freedom of individual entrepreneurs. So excessively individualist societies try, fortunately without complete success, to foster unlimited competition; not just *everyone for oneself*, but *everyone against everyone*.

In this framework, one must not restrain the powerful and greedy entrepreneur, such as Sam Walton or Rupert Murdoch, whose competition crushes his competitors. One must not pacify price wars which can threaten the viability of all those engaged in them, as one sees today in American civil aviation.

One must not discourage the investment bankers' frantic competition for the services of ace traders, which drives the remuneration of those traders to grotesque levels.

Nor must one restrain bankers from competitively expanding their lending business – even if that leads to excessive debts and widespread financial breakdown.

No Concern for the Common Good

Excessive individualism disapproves of public expenditure, of the diversion of personal riches towards the promotion of the common good. The promoters of this philosophy, armed with the theories of Mises and Hayek, argue that no individual, no organization, can possibly know what is best for the community. Hayek denounced *the persistence of instinctual feelings of altruism and solidarity*, those absurd and pathetic relics of the pre-libertarian past.[22]

Who alone, then, according to the extreme individualists, possesses the knowledge of what is best for society? Not you, not I, neither the church nor the town hall, certainly not the government.

---

[22] Friedrich von Hayek, THE FATAL CONCEIT (London: Routledge, 1988), 64.

None of those, but rather the impersonal aggregate of all us individuals, acting independently, heedless of the consequences for others of our actions, acting each for his or her own advantage.

In other words, His Majesty King Market in all his glory. As I have written elsewhere, *the sum of our independent actions becomes our god.*[23]

ANOTHER PENDULUM SWING?

The history of the interplay between the spirit of individualism and that of solidarity demonstrates that human societies find it hard to strike an acceptable balance between the prerogatives of the individual and those of the community. The exaggerated pursuit of individualism is reprehensible for two reasons. Its direct consequences can be very harmful, but that is not all; the bad consequences tend to provoke extreme reactions.

There is a risk that in the coming years people will become so disgruntled with the nasty results of several decades of libertarianism that we shall see once again an upsurge of some new variety of fascism, as suggested some years ago by Edward Luttwak in his famous essay, "Why Fascism is the Wave of the Future."[24]

Should this happen, part of the blame will lie with those who have promoted negative freedom and deregulation with such misguided enthusiasm.

---

[23] Angus Sibley, "From Calf to Market," THE MONTH (London, August 1998), 319; also on *www.equilibrium-economicum.net* (accessed 21 Oct 2010).
[24] Edward Luttwak, "Why Fascism is the Wave of the Future," LONDON REVIEW OF BOOKS (London), 7 April 1994.

POSITIVE OR NEGATIVE
FREEDOM?

Aristotle conceives freedom as the capacity to direct oneself to those ends
which one's reason rightly recognizes as choiceworthy.
MOIRA M. WALSH [1]

The possibility of sinning is not freedom, but slavery.
POPE LEO XIII [2]

Far from being straightforward and self-evident, the meaning of freedom
has always been and remains ambiguous and contested.
ANATOLE LIEVEN [3]

T he roots of exaggerated individualism and its cousin, anarchism, are closely entwined with certain misconceptions about the nature of freedom. Though the idea of freedom appears simple, it is in fact complex, because the word *freedom* has many distinct meanings. We all want to be free, but what kind of freedom do we want? What kind of freedom do we truly need? What kind of freedom is realistic, practical, desirable?

---

[1] Moira M. Walsh, "Aristotle's Conception of Freedom," JOURNAL OF THE HISTORY OF PHILOSOPHY, October 1997, 495-507.
[2] Pope Leo XIII, encyclical LIBERTAS PRAESTANTISSIMUM (1888), Par. 6.
[3] Anatole Lieven, "American freedom is a divisive concept," FINANCIAL TIMES (London), 7 August 2000.

Do we seek political freedom, religious freedom, personal freedom, national freedom? Freedom of speech or freedom of enterprise? To be free from stress, from violence, from pain, from hunger? *Negative freedom* (absence of constraints); or *positive freedom* (opportunity and possibility)?

POSITIVE CONCEPT OF FREEDOM

The Catholic Church has clarified the problem by defining 'true freedom' in the CATECHISM OF THE CATHOLIC CHURCH: *there is no true freedom except in the service of what is good and just.*[4]

The Social Dimension of Freedom

Thus, to achieve this true freedom one must pursue, in one's own behavior, goodness and justice. One must not be the slave of one's own sins. It is clear, however, that the good and just person may be oppressed by others and may in this respect lack freedom. It follows that, to be truly free, one must not only pursue goodness and justice, one must also be surrounded by others who do likewise, since they will not behave oppressively.

One does not achieve this true freedom merely by one's own virtue (save in the extreme case of Robinson Crusoe alone on his island); one needs the cooperation of others. True freedom is therefore not only an *individual* quality; it is also a *social* quality. This social aspect of freedom is well captured by the nineteenth-century English communitarian philosopher Thomas Hill Green:

---

[4] CATECHISM OF THE CATHOLIC CHURCH, Second Edition (Città del Vaticano: Libreria Editrice Vaticana, 1997), Par. 1733.

Freedom is a positive power or capacity of doing or enjoying something worth doing or enjoying, and that too, something that we do or enjoy in common with others.[5]

It has been said that *most of all, Green holds that the true good is a common or social good.*[6]

Catholic Theology of Freedom

A positive and virtuous conception of freedom is in tune with fundamental Catholic theology. Scripture speaks of the *slavery of sin* and pardon is called 'redemption' – a word that derives from the Latin *emptum*, meaning 'buy.' Redemption is thus equivalent to *buying out* or *buying back*, which in Biblical times meant buying a slave out of bondage, or ransoming a hostage.

It follows that freedom, in the Catholic sense of the word, is essentially the *opposite* of sin. Moreover, theology teaches that in heavenly eternity, where there is no sin, there is found perfect freedom. In the striking words of St Thomas, *inability to sin does not diminish our freedom;*[7] or, as St Augustine has it,

in the future life it shall indeed not be in man's power to will evil; and yet he shall not lack free will. In fact, his will shall be much more free once he is no longer in any way able to be the slave of sin.[8]

For another description of true freedom we may turn to the modern Catholic theologian Bernard Häring:

---

[5] Thomas Hill Green, WORKS OF T.H. GREEN, ed. R.L. Nettleship (London: Longmans, 1895 – 1911), Vol. III, 372.

[6] Maria Dimova-Cookson and W.J. Mander, T.H. GREEN: ETHICS, METAPHYSICS AND POLITICAL ECONOMY (Oxford: Clarendon Press, 2006), 10.

[7] St Thomas Aquinas, SUMMA THEOLOGICA, Secunda Secundae, Q. 88, Art. 4 (my translation).

[8] St Augustine, ENCHIRIDION, sect. 105 (my translation).

in its essence, freedom is the power to do good ... the power to do evil is not of its essence.[9]

The Error of Hayek

This may seem surprising to some of us, who too often imagine that freedom necessarily implies the possibility of doing wrong, as the atheist Austrian economist Friedrich von Hayek insists: *freedom is an opportunity to do good, but this is so only if it is also an opportunity to do wrong.*[10] But if we think like this, it is we who are mistaken and not St Thomas.

Our power to do evil is our power to choose between serving God and disobeying Him. That is not at all the same thing as the 'true freedom' defined in the Catechism. The choice between good and evil does not exist in heaven; on passing the pearly gates, we renounce it; and in renouncing it, we become truly free. A famous old prayer in the Anglican liturgy addresses God with the words *in whose service is perfect freedom.*[11]

In this world, on pilgrimage towards those gates, we do not achieve complete freedom; that is the goal towards which we are striving. The former French minister of education Xavier Darcos recently made this point very well: *in May 1968 many people thought wrongly that freedom should be our starting point; but in fact it is our*

---

[9] Bernard Häring, THE LAW OF CHRIST [*Das Gesetz Christi, 1951*], trans. E. G. Kaiser (Cork: Mercier, 1961) Vol. I, 99.

[10] Friedrich von Hayek, THE CONSTITUTION OF LIBERTY (London: Routledge & Kegan Paul, 1960), 79.

[11] "Collect for Peace at Morning Prayer," BOOK OF COMMON PRAYER (New York: Church Hymnal Corporation and Seabury Press, 1977), 57. This phrase is translated, somewhat loosely, from an ancient Latin prayer, which has at this point the words *cui servire regnare*, (whom to serve is to reign). The translation treats freedom as being equivalent to reigning, i.e., having power; clearly a very positive notion of freedom.

point of arrival.[12] To verify St Thomas' proposition, recall that often, on hearing of some outrageous crime, we react by asking: *how can anyone do a thing like that? I simply couldn't!* Do you feel that you are unfree, because you feel unable to commit some horrific atrocity?

Not likely! Inability to do something gravely wrong is not normally seen as a lack of freedom. The real eternal freedom, that of heaven, means inability to engage in any wrongdoing, great or small, monstrous or trivial. In Catholic theological terms, it is a basic error to claim that the power to do wrong is a freedom. One might as well claim that the right to sell oneself into slavery (which was possible and legal in Biblical times) was a freedom!

Affinities with Classical Philosophy

All this relates to what philosophers call the idea of *positive liberty*, the beneficent and creative power to do what is good and just. This Christian concept has affinities with classical Greek philosophy. Thus Aristotle, in a striking passage in the POLITICS, deplores certain democracies where

> ... *there has arisen a false idea of freedom which is contrary to the true interests of the State ... everyone lives as he pleases, or, in the words of Euripides, 'according to his fancy'. But this is all wrong; men should not think it slavery to live according to the rule of the constitution, for it is their salvation.*[13]

Freedom, or the opposite of slavery, is found in a life willingly directed towards the good of the republic, inspired by a shared

---

[12] Xavier Darcos, interview, LE MONDE (Paris), 1 June 2006.
[13] Aristotle, POLITICS, Book V, 136 (1310a).

understanding of goodness. As the French philosopher Jean-Claude Milner has observed, *freedom is an activity*.[14]

NEGATIVE CONCEPT OF FREEDOM

However, since the Reformation and the Enlightenment, many philosophers have turned away from the traditional positive conception of freedom. They have, to a greater or lesser degree, preferred the negative conception, which we may describe as *the freedom of the individual to act without constraints imposed by others and in whatsoever manner one thinks fit*, within the framework of a basic skeleton of fundamental laws, but without being subject to detailed particular regulations.

Negative Economic Freedom

In economics, the doctrine of negative freedom leads to the belief that business contracts, trading activities, etc. should not be regulated by the state; nor should they be regulated by associations of businesses or of workers (this latter kind of regulation is known as *corporatism*). Instead, the individual entrepreneur should, subject to certain basic legal principles, be free to be act as one pleases. This idea goes back to the eighteenth-century 'classical' economists, of which Adam Smith (1723–1790) and his French near-contemporary François Quesnay (1694–1774) are recognized as the earliest.

To be fair, we must remember that Smith did not believe that personal or commercial negative freedom meant indifference to

---

[14] Jean-Claude Milner, interview, *L'acte politique, ce sont les corps parlants*, LE MONDE, (Paris),
5 February 2011, 20.

the common good. That attitude is a morbid development that came later.

In his first major book, THE THEORY OF MORAL SENTIMENTS, Smith wrote that *the wise and virtuous man ... is willing that his own private interest should be sacrificed to the public interest.*[15]

Hayek's Claim of Negative Freedom

Hayek gives us one of the most uncompromising utterances of the negative conception of freedom:

> *Some philosophers have defined freedom as action in conformity with moral rules. But this definition of freedom is a denial of that freedom with which we are concerned. The freedom of action that is a condition for moral merit includes the freedom to act wrongly.*[16]

From a Catholic standpoint, this argument is easily refuted. Merit is earned by 'good works' rather than simply by not doing wrong.[17] Therefore, it is illogical to say that we can have no merit unless we are free to act wrongly. Thus Hayek rejects explicitly the link between freedom and virtue. With him, freedom loses contact with goodness and justice, becoming simply the absence of constraints imposed by other people. This is negative freedom in its pure, undiluted form.

Libertarians promote the idea that deregulation is intrinsically and always desirable.

---

[15] Adam Smith, THE THEORY OF MORAL SENTIMENTS (1759), ed. D. D. Raphael and A. L. Macfie (Oxford: Clarendon Press, 1976), 342.

[16] Hayek, THE CONSTITUTION OF LIBERTY, 79.

[17] See CATECHISM OF THE CATHOLIC CHURCH, Pars. 2006-2011.

This is an error based on the belief that freedom means the power to do wrong, as well as the power to do good; that, therefore, if people are to be free, we must refrain from trying to prevent them from doing wrong.

Isaiah Berlin's Repudiation
of Positive Freedom

The most famous modern repudiation of the positive conception of freedom is due to Sir Isaiah Berlin (1909–1997), a philosopher of Russian-Jewish origin who spent his academic career at Oxford, where he was professor of social and political theory.

In 1958 he gave a famous lecture, "Two Concepts of Liberty,"[18] and, since that dazzling fireworks-display of erudition, the classical positive concept has never quite recovered. Berlin argued that the notion of positive freedom is dangerous, for the following reason.

If freedom is to be found in the pursuit of ends that are good, just and reasonable, then it may happen that a government will identify and define a unique set of objectives that are said to have these qualities, and proceed to impose these objectives on everyone, arguing that, in furthering these good ends, everyone will be positively free. *We are making you free by obliging you to collaborate with our good projects.* No doubt the ultimate example of this lie is the phrase *Arbeit macht frei*[19] as it was abused by the Nazis.

---

[18] Isaiah Berlin, FOUR ESSAYS ON LIBERTY (Oxford: University Press, 1969), 118 – 172.
[19] Meaning 'work liberates,' this slogan is notorious for having been posted over the gates of several Nazi concentration camps. It does however have better associations. It originated as the title of a novel published in 1873 by Lorenz Diefenbach, whose hero, a fraudster and gambler, regains the path of virtue through regular employ-

POSITIVE FREEDOM
NEED NOT BE COERCIVE

So, according to Berlin, the logic of positive freedom leads towards totalitarianism. This argument has been taken up enthusiastically by Hayek and other libertarian theorists. Modern economic and political doctrine has thus been heavily colored by the dread of dictatorship that, for obvious reasons, has been a major preoccupation since the early twentieth century. However, Berlin's argument appears to be faulty, for two reasons.

Freedom in Choice

First, the classical positive concept of freedom implies that we find freedom by *choosing* to pursue good ends. Following Fr. Häring's definition, freedom is the power to do good, not compulsion to do good. Otherwise we would have the absurdity of a citizen of Aristotle's Athens telling his slave, *I am setting you free by making you do good work.*

A state may sometimes be justified in instructing and obliging its citizens to do good things, but the state does not thereby increase its citizens' freedom. If the state wants to help its citizens to be freer, it must try to expand their opportunities to do good things, for example by promoting better education or healthcare.

Libertarians argue that the state can enhance the freedom of its citizens by abolishing regulations. This may be true in cases where existing regulations are needlessly severe and restrictive, or where regulations clearly inhibit good as well as bad actions. But recent

---

ment. The phrase was also used by the German 'Weimar' government (1919-1933) to commend its program of public works projects aimed at reducing unemployment.

events in the financial world have shown how dangerous it is to remove too many regulations; in doing so, one opens the door to intolerable levels of misbehavior. And I have argued that the power to misbehave is not freedom.

Many Choices

Second, the theory of positive freedom does not in any way depend on the assumption that there is a unique system of good and just objectives. There may be many such systems. Berlin was afraid that the pursuit of positive freedom might force all individuals into a single mould, something that particularly horrified him because he was an ardent individualist. But there is nothing in the theory of positive freedom that requires everyone to pursue the same forms of goodness and justice.

Paradoxically, free-market economics has had in practice the effect of forcing more and more of our economic activities into a single mould. In the past, businesses took a wide variety of forms: public companies, state enterprises, cooperatives, private partnerships, mutual organizations, etc. The era of economic liberalization has seen the decline of most of these and the increasing dominance of one particular format: the limited company whose shares are quoted on a public stock market.

It is only fair to recognize that the philosophy of Berlin and of many of his contemporaries was dominated by horror at the appalling totalitarianisms of the mid-twentieth century and the need to avoid any repetition of such abuses. But it is surely wrong to reject a good and positive definition of freedom on the ground that it is possible for politicians to twist and pervert it. Bad politicians can twist anything. The remedy is to throw them out or, better, to prevent them from acquiring power in the first place. We should not allow their lies to pollute our philosophy.

4

BACKGROUND
TO AUSTRIAN ECONOMICS

---

*The German Historical School proposed the innovative historical-
ethical method and emphasized empiricism against rationalism, and
morality against self-interest. This does not mean the denial of
theory,but the demand for a new theory.*
YUICHI SHIONOYA [1]

A ustrian economics aimed to revive and advance the 'classical' economics of Smith and his successors, which, in
continental Europe in the mid-nineteenth century, had become
somewhat moribund, and had been overshadowed by the development of the contrasting German Historical School. Since the
Austrian economists saw themselves in opposition to what they
considered German heresies, we must examine in a little detail the
Historical School against which the Austrians reacted.

ADAM SMITH AND
THE BRITISH CLASSICAL SCHOOL

The history of the modern economic dialectic (conflict of contrasting doctrines) that concerns us goes back at least as far as

---

[1] Yuichi Shionoya, THE SOUL OF THE GERMAN HISTORICAL SCHOOL (New York: Springer, 2005), 10. The author is emeritus professor of economics, University of Tokyo.

Adam Smith. Although he was certainly not the first economist, he is generally recognized as the founder of modern economic science.

But Smith was in the first place a moral philosopher. He was professor of moral philosophy at Glasgow University between 1752 and 1764, before he began to write his economic masterpiece, THE WEALTH OF NATIONS (1776); and, during his Glasgow years, he published an important work, THE THEORY OF MORAL SENTIMENTS (1759).

He considered this book, as well as THE WEALTH OF NATIONS, as parts of a greater, very ambitious synthesis which he never completed. This was to include

> ... *an account of the general principles of law and government, and of the different revolutions they have undergone in the different ages and periods of society.*[2]

The Mechanical Model of Newtonian Physics

Clearly, Smith did not see economics as an isolated, self-contained theory. His economic writings, which abound in fascinating practical illustrations, were closely linked with his historical and philosophical studies. However, Smith shared the highly rationalist attitudes of his time. In an early essay, "The History of Astronomy," he acknowledged with lavish admiration the enormous influence of the theories of Isaac Newton:

---

[2] Adam Smith, THE THEORY OF MORAL SENTIMENTS (1759), ed. D D Raphael and A L Macfie (Oxford: University Press, 1976), 342.

The Newtonian system has received the general and complete approval of humanity, so that it must be considered as the greatest discovery ever made...the discovery of an immense chain of the most important, the most sublime truths, all closely linked by a single basic fact, whose reality we possess in our daily experience. [3]

The 'single basic fact' is Newton's law of gravity, namely:

The gravitational attraction between two objects is proportional to the product of their weights, and inversely proportional to the square of the distance between them. [4]

This simple principle was (until modern times with Einstein's theory of relativity) held to explain fully the movements of the celestial bodies. In the same way, Smith aimed to set up a 'system' to explain human economic behavior. As he wrote in the same essay,

a system is an imaginary machine, invented to connect together in the fancy those different movements and effects which are already in reality performed. [5]

So Smith set up his own 'imaginary machine' to explain the workings of the economy. The famous principle of the 'invisible hand' becomes the 'single basic fact' of economics, corresponding to Newton's law of gravity in astronomy. However Smith, as a practical man, recognized that the invisible hand did not, in the

---

[3] Adam Smith, final sentence of his HISTORY OF ASTRONOMY. This essay was unpublished in Smith's lifetime, and its date is uncertain. However, it must be prior to 1758, since it contains the remark that, according to astronomers' predictions, Halley's Comet is due to reappear in that year; as indeed it did. See Adam Smith, ESSAYS ON PHILOSOPHICAL SUBJECTS, ed. W P D Wightman and J C Bryce (Oxford: Clarendon Press, 1980), 105.

[4] See, for example, *http://zebu.uoregon.edu/~soper/Orbits/newtongrav.html* (accessed 21 October 2010)

[5] Smith, ESSAYS ON PHILOSOPHICAL SUBJECTS , 64.

real world, always produce good results. He admitted that, in certain circumstances, interference by the state was necessary.[6]

The Mechanical Philosophy in Smith's Successors

The economists of the *classical school*, Smith's successors, likewise insisted that their theories were universal principles. They claimed to have discovered laws analogous to those of Newtonian physics, and therefore valid at all times and in all places. We see, for example, this attitude in the distinguished French neoclassical economist Léon Walras (1834-1910), writing in 1900:

It is now quite certain that political economy, like astronomy, like mechanics, is a science at once experimental and rational … in the twentieth century … mathematical economics will take its place beside astronomy and mathematical mechanics; and then we shall have our just reward.[7]

This idea is now so widespread that today, more than two centuries after Smith, we find it even among left-wingers: *the law of the market is like the law of gravity.[8]* Who said that? Olivio Dutra, a leading trade unionist and leader of the political Left in Brazil. He evidently knows his Adam Smith – or, perhaps, his Walras.

The classical school of economics, which developed during the early decades of the 19th century, though it was based on Smith's ideas, tended to become isolated from other disciplines and from practical reality. The French historians Gide and Rist explain, in their classic history of economic doctrine:

---

[6] See, for example, THE WEALTH OF NATIONS, Book IV, chap. 2.
[7] Léon Walras, ELEMENTS D'ÉCONOMIE POLITIQUE PURE (1874-1877), Preface to the Fourth Edition, of 1900 (Paris: Pichon, 1952), final paragraph.
[8] Olivio Dutra made this comment at the 2005 World Social Forum, Porto Alegre, Brazil. See LE FIGARO ENTREPRISES (Paris), 7 February 2005.

With the successors of Jean-Baptiste Say[9] and David Ricardo,
political economy took on a more and more abstract character ...
it became stuck in a body of unappealing doctrines whose con-
nection with economic reality is more and more difficult to
perceive.[10]

The 'discovery' of 'natural laws' of economics led the economists of the classical school into the famous, and still current, practice of *mathematical modeling*: the construction of theoretical, often
very complex, models to represent the real economy, and thus to
predict its reactions to political actions or to natural events. But to
make these models work, one has to adopt the hypothesis that the
human actors in this mathematical drama act according to fixed,
logical and coherent motives.

Here we have a narrow and inadequate view of human psychology. Thus, as Gide and Rist remark,

Smith, Say, and Ricardo consider that man is motivated only by
his own interests. They imagine him totally absorbed in the pur-
suit of gain.[11]

CHALLENGE FROM
THE GERMAN HISTORICAL SCHOOL

Against this mechanistic vision of human nature and the
economy appeared the *Historical School* of economists, mainly in
Germany. Notable among the first 'historicists' were Wilhelm
Roscher, Karl Knies and Bruno Hildebrand; later Gustav Schmoller

---

[9] Jean-Baptiste Say (1767-1832), a French economist of the classical school.
[10] Charles Gide & Charles Rist, HISTOIRE DES DOCTRINES ECONOMIQUES (1909) (Paris:
Dalloz, 2000), Book IV, 426.
[11] Ibid., 443.

became, and long remained, the standard-bearer of this movement.[12]

Rejection of Mechanical Laws

These historicists based their analysis on human psychology
and on the study of historical experience, rather than on assumed
'laws' of human economic behavior. Some of them denied outright
that there could be any such laws; thus Hildebrand reproached
Roscher for having even admitted that economic laws existed.

An amusing tale is told about Schmoller. At a lecture given in
Geneva by the Italian neoclassical economist Vilfredo Pareto, who
spoke about such laws, Schmoller more than once interrupted Pareto by standing up and shouting that *there are no laws of economics.*
This odd behavior by a highly-respected middle-aged professor
illustrates how acrimonious was the dispute between the neoclassical and Austrian economists, who believed in the existence of
universal laws, and the German historicists, who did not believe.

Deduction versus Induction

In philosophical terms, the classical economists, and their later
followers, the neoclassicals and Austrians, have favored the method of *deductive reasoning.* One sets up certain hypothetical, or
axiomatic, principles, from which one deduces what will happen
in practice, given certain preconditions and certain actions or
events. By contrast, the historical economists preferred the method
of *inductive reasoning.* One observes economic facts as they have

---

[12] Translations from German Historical economists are my own. English translations
of these authors are generally nonexistent, such is the neglect of their ideas in the
Anglo-Saxon world.

emerged over the course of history; from these observations one infers (induces) certain underlying principles.

Broadly speaking, we can say that the classical and neoclassical economists have tended to see economics as comparable with astronomy, the science of celestial bodies which move predictably according to mathematical laws; while the historicists have seen economics as a discipline more akin to history and to psychology.

Pioneers of Historical Economics

Wilhelm Roscher (1817-1894), professor at Leipzig, did not deny the existence of economic laws. But he considered these laws to be entirely different from those of natural science, in that economic laws relate to free human beings endowed with reason, and thus with varying motivations for their actions. He argued that economic behavior varied between peoples, partly because of their differing cultures and ethnic characteristics, but also because of their differing levels or 'stages' of economic development. This is known as the *stage theory*. Thus Roscher wrote in his *Principles* that

> ... *like every form of existence, the life of a nation forms an entity whose diverse phenomena are intimately connected with each other. To scientifically understand one aspect thereof, one must understand them all; one must therefore pay attention especially to the language, the religion, the art, the science, the law, and the state, as well as to the economy.*[13]

Bruno Hildebrand (1821-1878), professor at Berne and later at Jena, called likewise for a holistic view of economics:

---

[13] Wilhelm Roscher, DIE GRUNDLAGEN DER NATIONALÖKONOMIE [*Principles of Political Economy*] (Stuttgart: J C Cotta, 1864), 27.

Man, as a social being, is a child of civilization and a product of history ... His needs, his culture, his relations with material things and with other people are not unchanging; they differ geographically, transform themselves over the course of history and progress along with the totality of human culture. [14]

Karl Knies (1821-1898), professor at Heidelberg, complained that

private egoism, self-interest, plays such a significant role in the [orthodox or classical] theory of national economics. He regretted that self-interest has been brought into such an immediate and deeply longstanding relation with the method of obtaining the laws of national economics ... [and that] it has exercised such a conditioning influence on the whole position of our science. [15]

Surely a text for our times! Knies summed up his reaction to all this in a concise and caustic phrase:

Self-interest ... serves, so to speak, the public interest in its weakness but is dangerous in its strength [ist gemeinnützig so zu sagen in seine Schwäche und gefährlich in seine Stärke]. [16]

Gustav Schmoller,
a Dominant Influence in Germany

Gustav Schmoller (1838-1917), professor at Berlin between 1882 and 1913, was for a long time the leading personality in German economics. He founded in 1879 the *Verein für Sozialpolitik*, an influential group of economists who formed a forum for the dis-

---

[14] Bruno Hildebrand, DIE NATIONALÖKONOMIE DER GEGENWART UND ZUKUNFT [*The National Economy of the Present and Future*] (Frankfürt am Main: J Rütten, 1848), Vol. I, 29.

[15] Karl Knies, DIE POLITSCHE ÖKONOMIE (Braunschweig: Schwetschke und Sohn, 1853) Book I, 147 and 157.

[16] Ibid.

cussion of social and economic policies, and from time to time advised the imperial government.

Though the members of the *Verein* were mostly conservatives, in the traditional European sense, they were nicknamed *Kathedersozialisten* ("academic socialists" – the word *Katheder* here means a professor's chair), because they generally favored policies which entailed considerable state intervention in economic matters. The famous state pension scheme introduced by Bismarck in 1889 was inspired by the *Verein*.

In a recent essay for the Pontifical Academy of Social Sciences, José Tomás Raga Gil, professor at the Universidad de San Pablo, Madrid, offers the following comment:

> *From the outset, the Association* [Verein] *gave particular attention to work in its social context. Wage levels and wage improvement, the training of employees ... the working time, social security and social services ... were the areas where the Association promoted by these two economists* [Gustav Schmoller and Adolf Wagner] *was most active.*[17]

Given the dominant position of Schmoller in his time, we summarize here some of the most important features of his thoughts on economics. For Schmoller, the classical theory was far too simplistic:

> *It is childish to believe that one can find in the theories of Quesnay,*[18] *Turgot, Smith, Ricardo and John Stuart Mill any more than a first provisional attempt at a systematic science.*[19]

---

[17] José Tomás Raga Gil, "A New Shape for the Welfare State," PROCEEDINGS OF THE EIGHTH PLENARY SESSION (April 2002) (Città del Vaticano: Pontifical Academy of Social Sciences), part VII, 215.

[18] François Quesnay (1694-1774), an economist of the group known as the Physiocrats, was an early advocate of free trade and minimal state intervention.

This harsh judgment reflects Schmoller's view that classical economists were guilty of a gross oversimplification in assuming that human beings behave consistently according to clearly-defined natural laws like those of physics. He rejected the very idea of unchanging, universal economic principles. *There is not, and cannot be, a supreme unique law of the action of economic forces.*[20] In biting terms he accuses the classical school of a fault easily recognizable in the world of economics today:

> *The more its hollow theory departed from observation and from the needs of real life ... the more worthless were the productions of the classical school ... It finished, as a class weapon delivered by Mammon itself into the hands of the capitalists, as a clever toy for clever people in ivory towers, ignorant of the world.*[21]

He rejected the 'iron law of wages' of the classical economists (see Chapter 5) which in effect accepted as inevitable that workers' wages tend towards a level no more than that required for bare subsistence. By contrast, for Schmoller *it is progress when the lower classes demand meat, good clothes, decent lodgings, their share in intellectual culture.*[22] He scorned *the general theory that egotism, self-interest and the desire for personal acquisition ... are, by themselves, the foundations of political economy.*[23] On the contrary, he affirmed, echoing Knies, that *the naked acquisitive instinct, in itself, is bad, even deranging, from the economic point of view.*[24]

---

[19] Schmoller, GRUNDRISS DER ALLGEMEINEN VOLKSWIRTSCHAFTSLEHRE [*Principles of General Economics*] (Leipzig: Duncker & Humblot, 1900/04), Vol. I, 92.
[20] Ibid., 109.
[21] Ibid., 93.
[22] Ibid., 25.
[23] Ibid., 32.
[24] Ibid, 37.

He recognized (like Marx, whose ideology in general, however, Schmoller detested)[25] the value of work not only as a factor of production, but also as necessary for human well-being. *Man cannot do nothing but eat and make love; he needs other things to occupy his time and his soul*[26]... *all moral strength has its roots in work.*[27] He prized the spirit of community:

> *The selfish acquisitive instinct finds its necessary corrective in the lively sense of neighborliness and in the clear view that the prosperity of each member of the community depends closely on the prosperity of all, and that all depend together on how well or badly the local administration works.*[28]

He was concerned about the then current menace of communism, which he condemned as a *centralistic despotism.*[29] He favored a balance between the public and private sectors:

> *It is highly desirable that the public economy should not absorb the private, or vice versa. The pans of the scales must remain in balance; the increase in the power of the State and its finances cannot have lasting beneficent consequences without corresponding progress in the freedom of individuals, of associations, of local government, of other corporations of all kinds.*[30]

Adopting for a moment the habitual tone of American conservatives, he insisted that

---

[25] Concerning Marx, Schmoller made, among others, the following comment: *Marx was a pessimist, a fanatic of hatred, for his social thinking lacked any psychological and moral-political foundation.* See GRUNDRISS, vol. II, 539.

[26] Schmoller, GRUNDRISS, Vol. I, 21.

[27] Ibid., 39.

[28] Ibid., 315.

[29] Ibid., 392.

[30] Ibid., 322. Note Schmoller's emphasis on 'subsidiarity' (see pp 15-17 supra)

one must not multiply to excess the provision of free services by the community, if one does not want to lose all sense of personal initiative and responsibility.[31]

He favored a major economic role both for the state and for local government. But communal services such as water, gas, waste disposal ... *can without too much inconvenience be left in private hands* on condition that they are strictly controlled by the local authority; *otherwise, it is much too easy for the holders of these monopolies to make excessive gains, while providing very bad services for the public.*[32]

The education of children, he argued, is rightly entrusted to the local authority, since *otherwise only the richest could afford to pay a teacher.* Moreover, the local government is

... better placed than any other entity to provide ... courses for adults, schools of agriculture and industry, libraries, theatres, concert halls, gyms, sports grounds and parks.[33]

Other matters which can well be undertaken by the local or state government are

... assistance for the poor, the construction of hospitals and orphanages ... compulsory health insurance ... savings banks, pawnbroking, sometimes even banks and mortgage banks.[34]

Schmoller saw good reasons for nationalizing the railways:

Competition between railway companies represents a waste of national resources ... railway companies and their shares are speculative instruments on the stock exchange; they offer shareholders a means of prodigious enrichment; they allow wealthy

---

[31] Ibid., 320.
[32] Ibid., 319.
[33] Ibid., 319.
[34] Ibid., 319-320.

investors [Großkapitalisten] *to exercise political and economic domination over the State and the national economy.*[35]

We see Schmoller striving to hold in balance the need both for private enterprise and for public provision of services, while he stresses the need for diffusion of powers between the State, the local authorities, and other corporate bodies.

Here is a vision of a well-regulated mixed economy, which could provide well-being and security for its citizens, thus neutralizing the attractions of communism, already a cause for anxiety in Europe at the end of the nineteenth century. This vision has indeed been largely realized in modern post-war Germany with its federal structure, its balance between strong public, private and cooperative (mutual) economic sectors.

SUCCESSORS OF
THE HISTORICAL SCHOOL

The Historicists remained dominant in Germany through the latter decades of the nineteenth century and the first decades of the twentieth. Their rejection of the dogmas of the classical school gave them popular appeal in a period of European reaction against the evil effects of lightly-regulated capitalism.

The German Ordoliberals

Later, a group of German economists known as the *Ordoliberals*, though they were more market-friendly, took up many of the ideas of the Historicists. It was they who introduced the term *social market economy* (*die soziale Marktwirtschaft*), recognizing the impor-

---

[35] Ibid., 320.

tance of the market in a free society, while rejecting the 'capitalism of the jungle.'

The Japanese economist Naoshi Yamawaki explains the difference between Ordoliberals and neoliberals (libertarians):

> *Whereas neoliberals, who emphasized the importance of efficiency, paid little attention to the circumstances of workers and even regarded the trade union as unnecessary, the Ordoliberals, who intended to establish a harmonious relationship between efficiency and social justice, took the situation of workers seriously and attached much importance to union-management cooperation* [Mitbestimmung].[36]

These Ordoliberals (Walter Eucken, Wilhelm Röpke and others) acquired considerable influence in West Germany after World War II, and thus helped to shape the outstandingly successful German economy as we know it today.

The American Institutionalists

The Historicists also had their successors in America, some leading American economists having studied in Germany towards the end of the nineteenth century. These were known as the *Institutionalists*; leading names in this group were Richard T. Ely, Henry Carter Adams, Thorstein Veblen. Their views were considered orthodox in America until around 1920, when Austrian and neoclassical[37] opinions began to take over. But the late John Kenneth Galbraith (1908-2006) carried on the Institutionalist tradition.

---

[36] Naoshi Yamawaki, "Walter Eucken and Wilhelm Röpke," THE GERMAN HISTORICAL SCHOOL: THE HISTORICAL AND ETHICAL APPROACH TO ECONOMICS, ed. Yuichi Shionoya (Routledge: London & New York, 2001), 198. The author is professor of philosophy at the University of Tokyo.

[37] See the next chapter for an explanation of neoclassical theory.

In our own times we see a re-emergence of the ideas and attitudes of the Historicists with, among others, Jacques Généreux in France, Geoffrey Hodgson in England, Elinor Ostrom (Nobel prizewinner 2009) and James Kenneth Galbraith (son of John Kenneth) in America.

5

FOUNDERS OF
THE AUSTRIAN SCHOOL

Value is the importance that the individual good, or quantity of goods, attains for us, because we are conscious of being dependent on command of them for the satisfaction of our needs ... value does not exist outside the consciousness of men ... the value of goods is entirely subjective in nature.

CARL MENGER [1]

What the socialists want is, to speak plainly, for the workers to get under the wage contract more than their work produces, more than they could get if they were entrepreneurs in business for themselves.

EUGEN VON BÖHM-BAWERK [2]

A compromise with the classical doctrine is aimed at, by declaring that its teachings are valid only under conditions of a general equality of forces. Where this equality does not prevail, complete freedom can only result in disadvantage to the weak.

FRIEDRICH VON WIESER [3]

The long tentacles ... of the Austrian school reached far into the future from when most of them practised and have had a profound and, in my judgment, irreversible effect on how mainstream economists think in this country.

ALAN GREENSPAN [4]

---

[1] Carl Menger, PRINCIPLES OF ECONOMICS [*Grundsätze der Volkwirtschaftslehre, 1871*], trans.
J. Dingwall & B.F. Hoselitz (New York: University Press, 1976), 117 and 121.
[2] Eugen von Böhm-Bawerk, CAPITAL AND INTEREST [*Kapital und Kapitalzins, 1889*], trans. G.D. Huncke & H.F. Sennholz (South Holland, Illinois: Libertarian Press, 1959), Vol. I, 471.
[3] Friedrich von Wieser, SOCIAL ECONOMICS [*Theorie der gesellschaftlichen Wirtschaft, 1914*], trans. A.F. Hinrichs (New York: A.M. Kelley, 1967), 410.
[4] Alan Greenspan, testimony to the House of Representatives Financial Services Committee, 25 July 2000.

CARL MENGER
AND THE METHODENSTREIT

Carl Menger (1840-1921), professor at the University of Vienna and tutor to Rudolph von Hapsburg, the hapless young prince who died with his mistress at Mayerling, is recognized as the founder of the *Austrian School* of Economics. He was a great theoretician who made important contributions to our understanding of economic phenomena.

And, as noted earlier, he set off a long-running controversy between economists, known as *der Methodenstreit*, a bitter dispute with Schmoller and his colleagues which might seem today to belong to the dusty archives of academic history.

Not at all! On the contrary, this obscure conflict between professors, this *Match Wien gegen Berlin* (contest of Vienna against Berlin), has had major and often unhappy consequences in our present-day world. The economists of the Austrian School constructed a rocket with a very long fuse, which however never fizzled out; their rocket has taken off and exploded after a long delay, but with spectacular effect.

The aim of the Austrian project was to overturn the Historical School and return to the methods of the classical economists. The Austrians were determined to go back to *a priori* theory, in preference to the practical observation of historical events; to rely on deduction rather than induction, as explained by Mises:

The economist does not base his theories upon historical re-search, but upon theoretical thinking like that of the logician or the mathematician ... he does not learn directly from history.[5]

There is the essence of the *Methodenstreit* (quarrel over methods), pursued with much vigor by Menger, Schmoller and their respective followers.

As it happens, the Austrians were unable to get the better of the Germans in the short term; the historical method remained dominant in Germany for several decades and gave birth to subsequent movements such as *Ordoliberalism* in Germany and *Institutionalism* in America, as we have already noted.

Austrian theory is distinct from contemporary neoclassical theory, developed in recent decades by economists such as Milton Friedman, Gary Becker, George Stigler, Kenneth Arrow and Gérard Debreu. A major difference is that the Austrians rejected the idea that the behavior of the various groups of economic agents (workers, consumers, investors ...) can be predicted or modeled by the use of mathematical formulae. We show below the positions in this regard of three groups or 'schools' of economists that are, or have been, dominant during the past century and more:

- **Neoclassical (Chicago) School.** Economics has definite, universal mechanical laws, like those of Newtonian physics; economic behavior (of groups of people or entire societies) is based on self-interest and can be modeled and predicted mathematically.

---

[5] Ludwig von Mises, THE ULTIMATE FOUNDATION OF ECONOMIC SCIENCE (Princeton: Van Nostrand, 1962), 73.

- *Austrian School.* Economics has definite, universal laws, but they are not rigidly mechanical, since human behavior is unpredictable, though guided psychologically by the same individualistic self-interest; so mathematical models are of little use.

- *German Historical School.* There are no (or hardly any) universal economic laws. Economic behavior varies according to historical conditions, cultural influences, ethnic characteristics, etc., and is not necessarily based exclusively on self-interest.

Naoshi Yamawaki offers a caustic comment:

> *The neoclassical perspective deals with the ethical dimension of the economy merely from the viewpoint of efficiency. Neo-Austrian liberalism, which stands against a mechanical explanation of the economy, as shown in the neoclassical equilibrium theory, shares with neoclassical economics this ethical negligence.*[6]

During the first half of the twentieth century, the worldwide dominance of socialist and collectivist ideas left Austrian theory in the shade. Only in the 1970s did it emerge into daylight, thanks to the rise of individualism and the collapse of communism. Some who heard Friedrich von Hayek lecture at the London School of Economics in the 1930s recall that his ideas were then considered bizarre.

Half a century later these same ideas, based on the doctrines which Menger and his colleagues had preached in the 1870s, had

---

[6] Naoshi Yamawaki, "Walter Eucken and Wilhelm Röpke," THE GERMAN HISTORICAL SCHOOL, 199.

become orthodox. Observe the length of the Austrian fuse: a good hundred years.

Menger's Marginal Theory of Value

Menger's PRINCIPLES OF ECONOMICS (the 1871 *Grundsätze*) marks a break with then-current economic thought. Hayek recalls a statement attributed to Menger, that he had *written this book in a state of morbid excitement.*[7] He had, indeed, undertaken an intellectually exciting project; the question of whether or not it was soundly based is another matter. In his preface to PRINCIPLES OF ECONOMICS, Menger states that his aim is

> *a price theory based upon reality and placing all price phenomena (including interest, wages, ground rent etc.) together under one unified point of view.*[8]

One notes a certain intellectual arrogance in this claim – 'my unique theory explains everything' – as well as its offence against Catholic values. In Menger's theory, as in most economic theory today, wage rates are treated no differently from other prices. Wherefore Pope John Paul II in his social encyclical LABOREM EXERCENS castigated

> *... various trends of materialist and economic thought; for certain supporters of those ideas, work is understood and treated as a kind of 'merchandise' that the worker ... sells to the employer.*[9]

Here, as elsewhere in papal teaching, stands condemned a fundamental error of what this pope called 'economism': the habit by

---

[7] Friedrich von Hayek, "Introduction" to Menger's PRINCIPLES, 16.
[8] Menger, PRINCIPLES, 49.
[9] Pope John Paul II, encyclical LABOREM EXERCENS (1981), Par. 7.

most economists of regarding labor as no different from any other tradable commodity.

Menger is known particularly as being the first to explain in detail the *marginal theory of value*. This has proved a lasting replacement, in economic thought, for the old theory of Smith and his successors, which held that the value of any product is determined by the cost of producing it. Not at all, say the Austrians, the causation goes the opposite way; the product has value because someone wants to buy it. The producer incurs the cost of producing it, because he expects to sell it at a price in excess of his cost. In fact, this idea can be traced back well beyond Menger; for example, the English logician Richard Whately, Anglican archbishop of Dublin, had observed in 1831 that

> *it is not that pearls fetch a high price because men have dived for them; but on the contrary, men dive for them because they fetch a high price.*[10]

The value of a pearl is not primarily *objective* (the cost of getting it from oyster to jeweler's shop), but rather *subjective* (the price that buyers are willing to pay for it). A similar theory had already been propounded by the French cleric and philosopher Etienne Bonnot de Condillac in LE COMMERCE ET LE GOUVERNEMENT (1776).[11]

Menger's theory is more subtle than Whately's. It recognizes that an article does not have the same value for all potential buyers. To explain how a price emerges in a market where buyers val-

---

[10] Richard Whately, INTRODUCTORY LECTURES ON POLITICAL ECONOMY (1831), lecture IX, 47. See *www.econlib.org/library/Whately/whtPE9.html* (accessed 25 June 2010).
[11] Available in English as COMMERCE AND GOVERNMENT, trans. Shelagh Eltis (Cheltenham, England, and Northampton, Mass.: Edward Elgar, 1997).

ue the same thing differently, Menger used the example of horse-copers selling horses to farmers.[12]

For us, it is perhaps simpler to consider the Dutch flower-market, an auction with *decreasing* prices. The auctioneer (*veiling-meester*) starts a 'clock' which shows prices; starting at a high level, it descends until the price is low enough to attract bids from the florists (or wholesalers who sell on to them). Florists, with shops in widely varying locations, sell at somewhat differing prices, depending on the purchasing power of their customers. Thus, the florist from the most *chic* district of Amsterdam can offer the highest price for a given quantity of tulips. A big lot, comprising hundreds or thousands of flowers of the same grade, will often be divided among several buyers; normally, all the sub-lots sell at very similar prices. These will be close to the price that the florist (among those who actually buy) from the least affluent district is willing (can afford) to pay.

Hence we have Menger's principle, which we can thus summarize: *the value of any article in commerce is the price conceded by the buyer whose 'best price' is the lowest.* This buyer is called the *marginal buyer* and we say that *the price is formed at the margin.*

While this principle applies to markets where quantities of identical items are traded, the theory of 'subjective' value is also relevant to unique items such as antiques or works of art. It explains why objects can change hands at prices that bear no relation whatever to their cost of production.

Damien Hirst's *Golden Calf*, a bullock preserved in formaldehyde, was sold at Sotheby's (London) in 2008 for £10.35 million; in

---

[12] Menger, PRINCIPLES, chap. 5, passim.

2006, Christies (New York) sold three bottles of the Burgundy wine Romanée-Conti 1978 for $211,500.

Monopolistic vs. Competitive Selling

Menger examines the difference between sale by a number of sellers in competition (which is what he favors and assumes) and sale by a monopoly supplier. At the flower-market, if all the irises were sold by a single association of growers, then this unique seller would have the possibility of improving its revenue by restricting the quantity of irises sent to market. The reduction in quantity could be more than compensated by the higher price achieved. For example, a 10% cut in sales might push the price 20% higher; clearly a good deal for the association.

By contrast, if the various growers sell competitively, without any agreement between themselves, such a tactic is impracticable (unless one grower has an extremely dominant market position). A grower who wanted a 10% cut in sales would have to make, on his own, the full 10% cut; for, without a collusive agreement with his competitors, he could not rely on them to help by reducing their own sales. Even if he is the biggest iris grower in the region, supplying 20% of the local market, to achieve a 10% cut in total sales he would have to halve his own crop. He could hardly hope to gain by doing that.

Thus it appears that competitive selling generally eliminates the possibility of profiting from a deliberate restriction of supply. Now, whatever their differences, classical and neoclassical and Austrian economists all wholeheartedly agree that competition is an absolute good.

So Menger affirms that, in the situation we have described, *one of the most socially injurious outgrowths of monopoly* [verderblichste Auswüchse des Monopolhandels] *is removed by competition.*[13] For in an environment of free competition, a trader can only maximize revenue by selling as much as possible.

Encouraging Maximum Production and Consumption

Notice Menger's underlying assumption. He takes it as axiomatic that any arrangement that might restrict production and consumption is *socially injurious.* Competition must be good, because it provides incentives to maximize production and consumption.

This assumption may have made sense in 1870, when global population was around 1.4 billion (one fifth of its present level), pressure on natural resources was not a major problem, and much of the working population still lived in severe poverty. But today, global consumption of many resources seems to be running at more than sustainable levels.

The human race as a whole cannot continue to increase its consumption of everything. Yet we persist in cherishing an economic philosophy whose fundamental principles encourage maximum consumption, which damns any restriction thereof as *verderblich*: a nasty adjective that means pernicious, shameful, vicious, corrupt.

---

[13] Menger, PRINCIPLES, 223.

Implications for Pay

While Smith and other classical economists argued that the value of anything had a basic floor, namely its cost of production, the *marginalist* theory of the Austrians in effect smashes the floor. It is normal, among economists today, no longer to recognize the cost of production as the basis for value.

Instead, value depends only on consumer demand and therefore has, in principle, no minimum.

Consider how this theory works out in the world of work. With the classical economists, the price of labor (worker's wage) was based on the 'cost of production' of labor, that is to say the cost of its subsistence.

Thus Smith's English follower, David Ricardo, proclaimed the 'iron law of wages:'

> The natural price of labor is that price which is necessary to en-able the laborers, one with another, to subsist and to perpetuate their race, without either increase or diminution. [14]

Likewise Smith's friend Turgot, finance minister to Louis XVI, had already written that

> in every kind of labor it must, and does indeed, happen that the worker's wage is limited to that which is necessary to provide for his subsistence. [15]

---

[14] David Ricardo, PRINCIPLES OF POLITICAL ECONOMY (1817), THE WORKS AND COR-RESPONDENCE OF DAVID RICARDO, ed. P. Sraffa and M. H. Dobb (Cambridge, England: University Press, 1951), Vol. I, 93.

[15] Anne-Robert-Jacques Turgot, REFLEXIONS SUR LA FORMATION ET LA DISTRIBUTION DES RICHESSES (1769), trans. P.D. Groenewegen, THE ECONOMICS OF A.R.J. TURGOT (The Hague: Nijhoff, 1977), 46.

A harsh doctrine, but at least it provided a base for wage rates. With the Austrian economists, however, this base crumbles. Menger tells us that

> *neither the means of subsistence nor the minimum subsistence of a laborer can be the direct cause or determining principle of the price of labor services.* [16]

On the previous page Menger observes that *in Berlin, a seamstress working fifteen hours a day cannot earn what she needs for her subsistence.* [17] In the same chapter he lambasts *the agitation of those who would like to see society allot a larger share of the available consumption goods to laborers.* Those kind-hearted people, says Menger, are really demanding *nothing less than paying labor above its value.* [18] Tough though the classical economists had been on the working classes, the Austrians have found a way of being even tougher.

The problem is not that the marginal theory of value is wrong. On the contrary, it is generally considered to be a realistic and useful explanation of how prices are formed in a free market. The harshness of the Austrian theory of wages stems from the error of regarding labor as a commodity whose value is determined in the same way as that of oil, wheat or copper; an error clearly condemned by Catholic teaching.

Before proceeding to the most famous members of the Austrian school, Ludwig von Mises and his pupil Friedrich von Hayek, we look briefly at some of the ideas of Menger's two most prominent immediate successors.

---

[16] Menger, PRINCIPLES, 171.

[17] Ibid., 170.

[18] Ibid., 174.

EUGEN VON BÖHM-BAWERK

Böhm-Bawerk (1851-1914), a lawyer by training, was Austrian finance minister between 1893 and 1904; during the 1880s, when he was professor at the University of Innsbrück, he wrote his monumental work KAPITAL UND KAPITALZINS [Capital and Interest]. He is known for his development of Menger's theory of marginal prices, and for his own erudite theory of interest.

As minister of finance, he was a 'hawk' who insisted on maintenance of the gold standard, on balanced budgets, and on the reduction of industrial subsidies. He was accused in some quarters of stifling the growth of Austrian industries by his unwillingness to support the development of the public infrastructure.

In his economic thought, he displayed opinions in conformity with his politics. He was fiercely opposed to Marxism, rejecting utterly the notion that workers were exploited by capitalists, whose profits, according to Böhm-Bawerk, were no more than interest on capital, necessary because of the lapse of time between production and sale. His rancorous attitude to socialism is shown in the quotation at the head of this chapter. Elsewhere he fulminates that:

> *I hardly think that anywhere else [than in the socialist theory of exploitation] are the worst errors concentrated in such abundance ... frivolous, premature assumptions, specious dialectism, inner contradictions and blindness to the facts of reality.*[19]

It is worth noting a comment by Rudolf Hilferding, a rebellious pupil of Böhm-Bawerk's, who diverged towards Marxism:

---

[19] Böhm-Bawerk, CAPITAL AND INTEREST, Vol. I, 557.

Whereas for Böhm-Bawerk labor seems merely one of the deter-
minants in personal estimates of value, in Marx's view labor is
the basis and connective tissue of human society.[20]

Here we glimpse an abysmal gulf between Marxism and free-market theory. For the one, work is in itself a human necessity; for the other, it is no more than an input in the productive process, thus an article of merchandise like any other.

On this point, Catholic teaching sides with Marx rather than with Böhm-Bawerk. And it doubtless this feature of Marxism – this deep respect for the value of labor – that has earned it, despite its grave errors and glaring self-contradictions, such a strong and lasting attraction for many people.

FRIEDRICH VON WIESER

Friedrich von Wieser (1851-1926), friend and brother-in-law of Böhm-Bawerk, succeeded Menger in the chair of political economy in Vienna. He is considered one of the leading members of the Austrian school, yet his views were, in many respects, very different from those of the other Austrians whom we discuss here. These differences may well reflect the fact that he was strongly Catholic in background and in lifelong practice.

In his URSPRUNG UND HAUPTGESETZE DES WIRTSCHAFTLICHEN WERTES [Original Source and Basic Laws of Economic Value],[21] Wieser refined and developed Menger's subjective theory of value. But he seems to have considered this theory incomplete. He agreed

---

[20] Rudolf Hilferding, BÖHM-BAWERK'S CRITIQUE OF MARX [*Böhm-Bawerks Marxkritik, 1904*], trans. Eden & Cedar Paul, in KARL MARX AND THE CLOSE OF HIS SYSTEM, AND BÖHM-BAWERK'S CRITIQUE OF MARX (Philadelphia: Orion, 1984), 186.

[21] Vienna: Hölder, 1884.

that value is grounded in what consumers are willing to pay, but argued that the process of value formation is circular; the original consumers' subjective valuation determines the original production cost, but this cost then becomes the value which subsequent consumers are expected to pay.

Wieser did not share the libertarian, anti-statist attitudes generally associated with the Austrian school. He was an example of a better route that the Austrian economists might have followed, had they not been deflected, by the rise of Nazism, fascism and communism, towards the extreme anti-statism which we shall find in Mises, Hayek and most of all Rothbard.

In his SOCIAL ECONOMICS, Wieser proposes many ideas that have little in common with 'Austrian economics' as it is commonly understood. His position is summarized in one striking sentence:

> *That the state, as the historically evolved organ of the common power, is bound to take whatever measures may be at its disposal for the protection of the common interest against the despotic powers of capitalism, requires no further proof.*[22]

He is in sympathy with trade unions, while recommending that they avoid strike action wherever possible:

> *When a union enforces a wage-rate that allows the full marginal productivity, it has won a considerable success for its members. It counteracts the unhealthy consequences of the over-competition of unorganized workers on wages, as well as defeating agreements between entrepreneurs to control wages ... Unions ... would render their members the highest possible service, if by a judicious use of their power they should become the*

---

[22] Friedrich von Wieser, SOCIAL ECONOMICS, 415.

agents for an amicable determination of the wages that are eco-
nomically demanded.[23]

He welcomes state regulation to restrain capitalist misbehavior:

Capitalistic despotism still dominates wide fields of enterprise. If
its effects do not seem too outrageous, society is indebted to the
protective legislation of the state for this result ... The modern
policy of national economy has decisively repudiated the doc-
trine of non-intervention.[24]

Wieser calls, as we note at the head of this chapter, for a compromise with classical economic theory which would recognize its
practical limitations. He opposes the excessive concentration of
capital (*Großkapital,* picturesquely translated by Hinrichs as
'mammoth-capital') that can arise in the absence of state intervention:

In no small measure, the profits of mammoth-capital are un-
earned winnings, obtained without efforts of leadership...the
state may [in such cases] without fear of harmful results, take
energetic action against the capitalists.[25]

He favors progressive taxation of income, based on the idea
that higher levels of personal income satisfy 'needs of decreasing
intensity' and therefore have decreasing marginal utility to the
recipient;[26] it is therefore reasonable to tax these higher income
bands at heavier rates. He insists, however, that the state should
not attempt to eliminate inequalities.

---

[23] Ibid., 377-8.
[24] Ibid., 406 & 409.
[25] Ibid., 413.
[26] Ibid., 433.

Wieser's argument for progressive taxation resembles Pope John XIII's words in his social encyclical MATER ET MAGISTRA, *ut tributa pro civium facultate imperentur*,[27] which literally translated means that citizens should be taxed according to their ability to pay. The official English version is 'that the burdens be proportioned to the capacity of the people contributing',[28] which might perhaps be taken to imply a 'flat tax' strictly proportionate to income; however, the Latin text avoids any suggestion of strict proportionality.

Of the three Austrian economists described here, Menger and Böhm-Bawerk represent the continuing mainstream of the Austrian School, in sharp opposition to the German Historical School. Wieser, by contrast, represents a diversion from the mainstream which proved to be ephemeral. He not only rejected the classical school's mathematical treatment of economic phenomena; he also rejected the classical postulate of freedom of contract, on the practical ground that contracting parties are often unequal in strength and therefore tend to set up inequitable contracts.

> *The freedom of personal contract … is not that supreme blessing that the liberal school sought to portray … in view of the helplessness of the weak individual, the slogan of the liberal school, "laissez-faire, laissez-passer", becomes almost a mockery.*[29]

---

[27] Pope John XXIII, encyclical MATER ET MAGISTRA (1961), Par. 132.

[28] We may note that the 'capacity' of taxpayers (Latin *facultas*) varies (as a proportion of income) in relation to the taxpayer's total income; thus, for example, if we consider the top 20% slice of a taxpayer's income, it may well be easier, or no harder, to pay 40% ($8,000) of this slice from an annual income of $100,000, than to pay 20% ($400) of the same slice from an annual income of $10,000. Indeed, in the same place cited above (note 25) Wieser observes that *the present advanced point of view regards the payment of a tax levied upon a subsistence income as so oppressive that it should not be demanded under any circumstances.*

[29] Wieser, SOCIAL ECONOMICS, 379.

Wieser clearly favored state and trade union intervention to rectify the consequent injustices, as well as to mitigate inequalities.

His stance has not been followed by more recent Austrian economists, primarily because of the rise of totalitarian states in the early twentieth century. This led to the belief that it was vitally important, as a matter of basic strategy, to minimize state power, replacing it wherever possible with the 'spontaneous order' of the market. In this climate, the later Austrians felt that Wieser pointed in the wrong direction.

6

MISES' INTRANSIGENT INDIVIDUALISM

*Social problems were considered ethical problems. What was needed
to construct the ideal society, they thought, were good princes and
virtuous citizens ... The discovery of the inescapable interdependence
of market phenomena overthrew this opinion.*
LUDWIG VON MISES[1]

*A libertarian ideology which claims, in a manner strangely close to
that of the Stalinist gospel, to be in tune with the very nature of
things and to exclude all possible alternatives.*
NICOLAS WEILL[2]

LUDWIG VON MISES

L udwig von Mises (1881–1979) studied law (not economics)
at the Akademische Gymnasium in Vienna between 1900
and 1906; he also followed a private seminar given by Böhm-
Bawerk. It was, however, his reading of Menger that persuaded
him to become an economist.

---

[1] Ludwig von Mises, HUMAN ACTION (New Haven: Yale University Press, 1949), 2.
The past tense in the opening phrases refers to the era prior to the rise of 'subjectivist
economics' in the late nineteenth century.
[2] Nicolas Weill, "Althusser revient?," LE MONDE (Paris), 30 July 2008.

The subjective conception of value, developed as we have seen by Menger, became the foundation of Mises' thought. Like Hayek, Mises held statist views in his youth, but soon abandoned entirely this position. Mises' contempt for the practical economists of the German Historical School was so great that he refused to recognize them as economists. He argued that they did not deserve the name because they did not believe in the existence of universally valid economic laws.

> *Understanding [of diverse cultures] … does not permit the modern historian to state that an economic law was not valid in ancient Rome or in the empire of the Incas.*[3]

He apparently thought that if, like Roscher, Hildebrand, Schmoller and others, one argues that economic behavior varies according to race or culture, one becomes guilty of a kind of racism. He wrote that

> *Some ethnologists … are utterly mistaken in contending that … other races have been guided in their activities by motives other than those which have actuated the white race.*[4]

In contrast with economists of the 'classical' and 'neo-classical' schools, Mises was strongly opposed to the attempt to explain economic phenomena mathematically, to treat economics like physics. He insisted, nonetheless, that *economics, like logic and mathematics, is a display of abstract reasoning. Economics can never be experimental and empirical.*[5] Economic theory, he argued, is an *a priori* theory developed by means of deduction from certain basic axioms. his view lies at the very heart of Austrianism. In explicit refutation of the

---

[3] Mises, HUMAN ACTION, 68.

[4] Ibid., 84-85.

[5] Ibid., 868.

German historicists, Austrians insist that you cannot learn economics by observing what happens in real-life economies. You can only learn by reasoning from prior assumptions about human behavior.

Mises' book HUMAN ACTION, first published in 1949, in English, is considered his most important; another major work, DIE GEMEINWIRTSCHAFT [Socialism] dates from 1922. Dominant themes of his thought are:

- the primary importance of the free action of the individual
- the supreme virtues of the untrammeled market
- an absolute abhorrence of collectivism and socialism in all their forms

MAXIMIZING INDIVIDUAL LIBERTY

Mises' Theory of Action

The Austrian theory as defined by Mises constitutes a formal system of *praxeology*, a term invented by the French philosopher Alfred Espinas (1844-1922), from the Greek πραξις ('praxis,' meaning 'action'); it is defined by Mises as *the general theory of human action*.

Like his parents he was a non-religious Jew, and his theory expresses rather curious ideas about God. The foundation of this theory is a single axiom which we may summarize thus: *human action is directed towards ends defined by each individual, rather than being simply a response to external circumstances*. According to Mises, such purposeful action is something that belongs to man, but not to God: *the Almighty does not act ... it is anthropomorphism to attribute action to God.*[6]

The odd notion that 'God does not act', which would seem to be in total contradiction with Jewish and Christian theology, is related to Mises' peculiar definition of action, namely that one only acts if one is not content with one's present situation: *action can only be imputed to a discontented being ... if one were contented, one would not act.*[7]

Yet one can evidently act simply for the pleasure of acting, without any ulterior motive. This would not be action as defined by Mises. Nor could it possibly be work in Mises' sense of the word. We shall see later how this definition of action underlies Mises' negative attitude to work.

For Mises, in order that individuals should achieve the fullest possible self-realization, they must reserve to themselves the maximum liberty to act upon their own initiatives. We see here a similarity with Hayek's argument that the individual must be set free from constraints imposed by other people; though not from the constraints of impersonal mechanisms (such as the free market), which do not damage freedom as Hayek defines it.

Negative Freedom as
Foundation of True Civilization

Mises was utterly convinced that the human being cannot live freely except in a free-market *laissez-faire* economy; he therefore became a vociferous, and it seems fair to say bigoted, promoter of

---

[6] Mises, THE ULTIMATE FOUNDATION OF ECONOMIC SCIENCE (New York: Van Nostrand, 1962), 3.
[7] Mises, HUMAN ACTION, 69.

this ideology. So obsessed was Mises with the need for maximum 'negative freedom' for every individual, that he condemned the entire galaxy of Oriental civilizations, not known for their fondness for rigorous individualism, as having produced (during recent centuries) little or nothing of any cultural value. With blatant self-contradiction he thus fulminates:

> For many centuries the East has not generated any book of importance. The intellectual and literary history of modern ages hardly records any name of an oriental author. The East has no longer contributed anything to the intellectual effort of mankind … the reason is obvious. The East lacked the primordial thing, the idea of freedom from the state. The East never raised the banner of freedom.[8]

Yet Mises admits, in the same chapter, that:

> … the civilizations of China, Japan, India and the Mohammedan countries of the near East … already many hundreds, even thousands of years ago, brought about marvelous achievements in the industrial arts, in architecture, in literature and philosophy.[9]

Were they 'free' in the Misesian sense in those earlier times? Not according to Mises.

Again, in the same chapter, he insists that *what separates East and West is first of all the fact that the peoples of the East never conceived the idea of liberty.*[10] So how did they ever bring about those 'marvelous achievements'? Mises does not explain.

---

[8] Mises, THE ANTI-CAPITALISTIC MENTALITY (Grove City, Pennsylvania: Libertarian Press, 1990), 103.
[9] Ibid., 102.
[10] Ibid., 90.

Autonomous Choice and
Value-free Economics?

Mises, however, always insisted that his economic researches were *Wertfrei* (value-free); that is to say, in his work he refrained from making any value judgments. Yet his writings abound in virulent denunciations of his pet hates: statism, socialism, and virtually all forms of interference with the free market. Here is a paradox which, it seems, cannot really be resolved.

Mises argued that his conclusions were based on theoretical analysis into which no value judgments entered.

> *Economics ... is perfectly neutral with regard to all judgments of value, as it refers always to means and never to the choice of ultimate ends.*[11]

So, we are meant to understand that Mises is concerned purely with showing us the best way to achieve particular economic results (ends), without saying anything about which results are the most desirable. But the intensely polemical tone of his writing makes this implausible. Mises is always telling us what results we ought to want to achieve. Apparently he considered it axiomatic that these were the only acceptable results, that no reasonable person could possibly desire any others. This stance leads to a hectoring style of discourse; for example:

> *The choice is between capitalism and chaos ... Socialism is not an alternative to capitalism, it is an alternative to any system under which men can live as human beings.*[12]

---

[11] Mises, HUMAN ACTION, 884-5.
[12] Ibid., 680.

Mises' researches seek explicitly the most effective means to arrive at a definite goal, namely an economy that makes possible the fullest possible realization by the greatest number of individuals of subjectively chosen ends. He considers it axiomatic that this must be the best conceivable goal, on the ground that the ends chosen by individuals are without exception 'rational'. Mises indeed makes the astonishing statement that *human action is necessarily always rational*. Consequently, he continues,

> *Since nobody is in a position to substitute his own value judgments for those of the acting individual, it is vain to pass judgment on other people's acts and volitions.*

He concludes that

> *... our science, because it is subjectivistic and takes the value judgments of acting man as ultimate data not open to any further critical examination, is itself above all strife of parties and factions, it is indifferent to the conflicts of all schools of dogmatism and ethical doctrines, it is free from valuations and preconceived ideas and judgments, it is universally valid and absolutely and plainly human.*[13]

So, whatever choices are freely made by individuals are intrinsically 'right' in the sense that they are right for the persons making the choices. Others are obliged to accept these choices. Society has no right (except perhaps in criminal cases) to question or oppose these choices, whatever may be their effects upon society, because the individual is always entitled to act in his own best interest.

---

[13] Ibid., 21

But this hypothesis, that individual choices are always rational and socially 'acceptable', is surely debatable. The economist Giulio Palermo, in a thoughtful commentary on the Austrian doctrine, argues that, contrary to Mises' assertion, this hypothesis is in itself a value judgment, and he continues:

> That every individual is the best judge of his own well-being is a value judgment that seems easy to accept. Things are, however, not so simple. The debates on abortion and euthanasia, and the right or prohibition to use different kinds of drugs, are examples of the moral problems involved in this value judgment. [14]

One could well add to Palermo's little list the belief of many individuals that their well-being is strictly proportional to their purchasing power.

DEFENDING THE UNREGULATED FREE MARKET

Mises' Reductionist Definition of Human Work

Labor is a means, not an end in itself. [15] Mises rejects the notion that the worker may find a certain satisfaction in the execution of his work. He satirizes

> the superficial observers ... [who] think that the railroad engineer must enjoy operating and steering his engine as much they would if they were permitted to toy with it. [16]

---

[14] Giulio Palermo (Dept. of Economics, University of Brescia), "Are we all Keynesians?" HISTORY OF ECONOMIC IDEAS (Cambridge University Press), 2005/1; see also Sandye Gloria-Palermo and Giulio Palermo, "Austrian Economics and Value Judgments," REVIEW OF POLITICAL ECONOMY (Routledge, London), Vol. 17, No. 1 (January 2005).
[15] Mises, HUMAN ACTION, 131.
[16] Ibid., 138.

We may note in passing that Mises seems unaware of the fact that a locomotive on its rails has no need of being steered like a car or a ship.

This attitude (to work, not to locomotives) is normal among libertarian economists. They insist that work serves no purpose except to produce things that consumers want to buy. They ignore the principle that work is necessary for human well-being, that it can be in itself one of the means of self-realization. This notion is perhaps unacceptable to libertarians because of its Marxist associations; thus Marx complains that:

> ... it seems quite far from Adam Smith's mind that the individual, 'in his normal state of health, strength, activity, skill, facility' also needs a normal portion of work.[17]

Mises' Outdated View of Labor as Scarce

In HUMAN ACTION Mises lays down his principle of the scarcity of labor, which was possibly plausible during the 1950s and 1960s when unemployment was generally much lower than is usual today. This principle reflects an attitude not uncommon among free-market economists, which helps to explain some of their more unpalatable views:

> Labor is the most scarce of all the primary means of production because it is in this restricted sense nonspecific and because every variety of production requires the expenditure of labor ... on the labor market of a market society there are buyers for every supply of labor offered.[18]

---

[17] Karl Marx, GRUNDRISSE, Chapter on Capital, Notebook V (1858), trans. Martin Nicolaus (London: Penguin, 1993), 611.
[18] Mises, HUMAN ACTION, 135.

Mises provides no real proof of this assertion; he explains it by pointing out that work is necessary for all production, and by assuming that work is always a *disutility*, i.e., something we would rather not do. We would, it seems, always rather be idle than work. Labor is intrinsically scarce, because we work only unwillingly, under pressure of necessity, or of desire for more money.

Notice the relation with Mises' assumption that we do not 'act' (or work) unless we are dissatisfied with our present condition. Meanwhile, according to Mises, there are no serious scarcities of other resources; there are indeed *unused material resources*.[19] We need not hesitate, therefore, to stoke up sufficient growth to keep everyone employed.

However, Mises permits himself to imagine, for a moment, a quite different situation. In this brief but memorable passage he puts a large bomb under much of his own philosophy, to which is attached a long fuse which is still slowly burning, though in fact the bomb should have exploded years ago.

> *We may try to imagine the conditions within a world in which all material factors of production are so fully employed that there is no opportunity to employ all men, or to employ all men to the extent that they are ready to work. In such a world labor is abundant ... if it were a market society, wage rates paid would not be enough to prevent starvation. Those seeking employment would be ready to go to work for any wages, however low, even if insufficient for the preservation of their lives. They would be happy to delay for a while death by starvation. There is no need ... to discuss the problems of such a world. Our world is different. In our world there is no abundance, but a shortage*

---

[19] Ibid., 136.

of manpower ... this state of affairs could be changed by such an increase in population figures that all material factors required for the production of foodstuffs are ... fully exploited.[20]

When Mises published that, in 1949, world population was around 2.5 billion or 38% of its present level, and the danger of exhaustion of natural resources was not a widespread concern.[21] One need hardly point out that we have now entered an age wherein our overall consumption of natural resources is becoming unsustainable. Even if an apparent abundance of many resources is still *available,* it would be imprudent and irresponsible to continue to increase our overall consumption. We are thus witnessing the overturning of the situation described by Mises and its replacement by a *relative abundance* of labor.

We do indeed need to discuss the problems that Mises dismissed so curtly. No longer can we hope to eliminate unemployment by simply growing our economies in the conventional way; limitations on resources and the problems of pollution make that impossible. Mises himself has warned us that, in these circumstances, a free market in labor is not humanly tolerable.

Mises' Claim that Value is Purely Subjective

Mises, following Menger, was an unconditional supporter of the subjective theory of value. He expressed this belief in a striking phrase: *Value is not intrinsic, it is not in things. It is within us; it is the way in which man reacts to the conditions of his environment.*[22]

---

[20] Ibid.

[21] See *www.census.gov/ipc/www/idb/worldpopgraph.php* (accessed 21 October 2010).

[22] Mises, HUMAN ACTION, 96.

We have already examined (Chapter 4 above) two major difficulties with this theory. First, the subjective 'marginal' value, which Austrians consider the only true value, emerges only in conditions of untrammeled competition. And these conditions exclude in principle, as Menger explained, any deliberate restraint on quantities sold. In a world where overall consumption is becoming excessive, the objections to this regime are obvious.

Second, the application of the subjective principle to labor markets means that there is no basic floor for wage rates; nor, for that matter, is there any ceiling. The subjective principle is thus conducive to exorbitant inequalities. Mises showed little concern about this problem:

> *the inequality of incomes and wealth is an inherent characteristic of the market economy. Its elimination would totally destroy the market economy.* [23]

But the theory of subjective value is open to a more profound objection. Mises' attitude is clearly anthropocentric; it places the human rather than God at the center of the universe. Things created by God are said to have no value save in the estimation (market pricing) of us human beings. That smells of heresy, indeed of blasphemy, does it not?

Mises, as we have seen, was a non-observant Jew, and it is clear that his attitude to value is not Jewish, nor for that matter is it Christian or Islamic. But one does not have to be devoutly religious to see that there are grave practical objections to ascribing no value to anything that does not have a market price. We discard as worthless things that are not readily sellable, such as gas flared

---

[23] Ibid., 840.

from oil wells, materials that cannot be reused at an economic cost, machinery that is 'not worth repairing'.

My wife once, in a photographic shop in London, asked to have a camera repaired; the puzzled salesman replied with a memorable question: *repair, madam, what does that mean?* How many millions of tons of materials are junked yearly as a result of this attitude? All this in a world that is consuming many natural resources at unsustainable rates. Moreover, we human beings are crowding out plant and animal species that happen to have no current commercial value; another example of the consequences of failing to value that which has no market price.

SOCIALISM AS THE ONLY DANGER

Mises abhorred every aspect of 'socialism', even in its most moderate forms. The whole of Part V of DIE GEMEINWIRTSCHAFT is devoted to vitriolic attacks on each of its manifestations, all of which are branded collectively with the name of *Destructionism*. For, in Mises' view, any economic arrangements other than pure, unalloyed, unregulated capitalism are inevitably destructive of capital, and indeed of everything else: *Socialism … is the spoiler of what thousands of years of civilization have created.*[24]

Opposition to Social Welfare Programs

Legislation on conditions of employment is *the most harmless* form of destructionism, though it is objectionable in principle as a

---

[24] Mises, SOCIALISM [*Die Gemeinwirtschaft, 1922*], trans. J. Kahane (New Haven: Yale University Press, 1951), 458.

danger to industrial development; however Mises considers it generally inoffensive, because ineffective.[25]

Compulsory sickness insurance is condemned as *an institution which tends to encourage disease by weakening or completely destroying the will to be well and able to work.*[26] Moreover,

> *assistance of the unemployed has proved to be one of the most effective weapons of deconstructionism ... what the unemployed person misses is not work but the remuneration of work.*[27]

Notice how all this follows from Mises' insistence that work is always a disutility. Mises' working class, it would seem, is a race of incorrigibly lazy scroungers who will jump at any excuse to avoid going to work. In the same section we find a dire warning against *the great social dangers involved in any extension of poor relief.*[28] Elsewhere, Mises rants at tiresome length against the legal minimum wage, warning that *any mode of fixing minimum wage rates above the market height brings about institutional unemployment.*[29]

Opposition to Labor Unions

If, as Mises assumes, labor is the scarcest factor of production, then it follows that workers are in an inherently strong bargaining position; this allows Mises to argue that they have no need for trade unions, social insurance, or protective legislation. Unions, he says, are anyway fundamentally useless, because they can in no case improve wages without diminishing the demand for labor.

---

[25] Ibid., 473.
[26] Ibid., 477.
[27] Ibid., 484-5.
[28] Ibid., 475.
[29] Mises, HUMAN ACTION, 776.

There has never yet been a wage-theory from which one could deduce that association by means of trade unions led to a permanent increase in the real income of the workers.[30]

For, according to Mises, it is impossible to increase wages except by an increase in the productivity of labor. He thus excludes the possibility of any variation of the workers' share in the total revenue (gross domestic product or GDP) of a country. It is however well known that, in the USA over recent decades, though productivity and GDP have increased, workers in general have scarcely profited thereby, because the share of wages in GDP has declined in favor of shareholders' profits and top-level executive salaries.[31]

Mises treats labor as a commodity like any other, arguing that, if it becomes more expensive in real terms, then inevitably less of it will be bought (if wages rise, there will inevitably be more unemployment).

But this does not necessarily happen with other commodities. Over the forty years 1967-2007, crude oil prices have multiplied by just over 21, while the US cost of living has multiplied by just over 6.[32] Oil has thus become very much dearer (its price has more than tripled) in real terms. So, are Americans using less oil?

Certainly not. Consumption of petroleum products has risen from 12.6 million barrels per day in 1967 to 20.7 million in 2007.[33]

---

[30] Mises, SOCIALISM, 402.

[31] See WORLD OF WORK REPORT 2008 (International Labor Office), 6, on *www.ilo.org/public/english/bureau/inst/download/world08.pdf* (accessed 21 October 2010).

[32] See *http://inflationdata.com/inflation/Inflation_Rate/HistoricalInflation.aspx* (accessed 21 October 2010).

[33] See *www.eia.doe.gov/emeu/aer/ep/ep_frame.html* (figure 18) (accessed 21 October 2010).

Allowing for population increase, consumption has grown modestly, by 8.6% per capita; it clearly has not shrunk. Since oil producers have combined to demand higher prices for their crude, users have accepted that they have to pay more, and they pay. Likewise, if workers combine to demand higher wages, employers have to pay. Without effective cooperation (strong unions), workers in America have lost out to management and shareholders.

Claim that Free Markets Are True Democracy

Mises desired the replacement of the state, so far as practically possible, by the impersonal regulation of the free market. This reflected his view that *the capitalist society is a democracy in which every penny represents a ballot paper.*[34] He argued that the market reflects the people's wishes better than the electoral system, because we vote only every few years but spend money every day.

That is doubtless true, but the market inevitably responds better to the fancies of big spenders, than to the needs of those who can spend little. The Constitution offers us *one person, one vote*; in the market, it is *one dollar, one vote*. Instead of an option in favor of the poor, we have here a bias in favor of the rich. We discuss this point further in chapter 11.

Mises thus believed that 'democracy' should be achieved through consumer spending rather than through political process; this is the Austrian doctrine of *consumer sovereignty*, the idea that economy and society should be fashioned primarily and mainly by the way individuals spend their money. He provides a memorable description of this phenomenon:

---

[34] Mises, SOCIALISM, 443.

The captain is the consumer ... Neither the entrepreneurs nor the farmers nor the capitalists determine what has to be produced. The consumers do that...They are merciless egotistic bosses, full of whims and fancies, changeable and unpredictable. For them nothing counts other than their own satisfaction ... In their capacity as buyers and consumers they are hard-headed and callous, without consideration for other people ... Capitalists, entrepreneurs, and landowners can only preserve their wealth by filling best the orders of the consumers ... In the conduct of their business they must be unfeeling and stony-hearted because the consumers, their bosses, are themselves unfeeling and stony-hearted.[35]

Nothing in the context of this paragraph suggests that Mises is trying here to denigrate the consumer society. On the contrary, he is describing the free-market economy as he believes it naturally is and should be. To be sure, his words describe all too accurately how we tend to behave 'in our capacity as buyers and consumers'. We tend not to give very much thought to the interests of those who produce what we buy, of whom often we know little. All the more reason, one might think, why the economy should not be run solely in the interests of consumers.

Scorn on Redistribution

Like other libertarian economists, Mises pours scorn on the concept of redistribution. His main argument is that a progressive scale of taxation (higher rates on richer taxpayers) would stifle the growth of new businesses; it would destroy the incentive to accumulate capital or to earn maximum profits. He complains that

---

[35] Mises, HUMAN ACTION, 270-271

> *... today taxes often absorb the greater part of the newcomer's 'excessive' profits. He cannot accumulate capital; he cannot expand his own business; he will never become big business and a match for the vested interests. The old firms do not fear his competition; they are sheltered by the tax collector.* [36]

They are 'sheltered', according to Mises, because high rates of tax on business profits make it difficult for new firms to establish themselves. But this is an argument for having lower tax rates on the profits of small businesses, a practice followed in many countries, including the USA. In other words, a progressive scale of corporate income tax. Mises apparently considers profiteering a praiseworthy activity:

> *The greater the profits, the better the needs of the consumer are supplied. For profits can only be reaped by removing discrepancies between the demands of consumers and the previous state of production activities. He who serves the public best, makes the highest profits.* [37]

This argument would seem to be largely a triumph of theory over practical experience. But, then, as Mises insists, real economists learn from theory, not from history.

Claim that Free Markets Bring Peace

According to Mises, the free market is not only a near-miraculous generator of prosperity; it is also a guarantor of peace: *modern total war is a war against trade and migration barriers.* [38] Hence it follows that

---

[36] Ibid, 809.
[37] Ibid.
[38] Ibid, 824.

... laissez-faire eliminates the causes of international conflict ... what has transformed limited warfare between royal armies into total war, conflict between peoples, is ... the substitution of the welfare state for the laissez-faire state.[39]

So, it would seem, the major wars of modern times, including Hitler's war, have been caused by restrictions on free trade or on immigration, or by the introduction of social security. Today, the strange argument that welfare-state systems are inseparable from tyranny, imperialism and warmongering is a staple commodity in American libertarian circles, particularly among members of the Ludwig von Mises Institute.[40]

It is argued, more or less correctly, that the hated practices of the paternalist welfare state were first introduced by Otto von Bismarck, the Prussian leader who was chancellor of the German empire from 1871 to 1890, among whose advisors were the economists of the *Verein für Sozialpolitik* (see Chapter 3). Since the Bismarck period was followed by the more bellicose regimes of Kaiser Wilhelm II and later Hitler, it is further argued *post hoc ergo propter hoc*[41] that the great wars of twentieth-century Europe were the results of Bismarck's welfare policies; or, more precisely, of the degree of state control that was necessary to implement those policies.

Well, one may argue that Bismarck pioneered the benevolent state because he wanted the German people to be loyal supporters

---

[39] Ibid., 823-824.
[40] See, for example, Anthony Mueller, "Bye-bye, Bismarck" on *www.mises.org/daily/1275* (accessed 26 June 2010).
[41] Meaning "after this, because of this" and referring to the logical fallacy that, because a subsequent event follows a prior one, the prior event must be the cause of the subsequent one.

of his government, and that such loyalty, once established, was abused by the Kaiser and by Hitler. But what would have been the alternative to Bismarck's policies? He was driven by the fear that disaffected Germans, sick of the ugly consequences of raw capitalism, might turn to communism. Would early twentieth-century Germany have been less aggressive under a communist régime?

In the nineteenth century, Britain and France and some other European countries followed aggressive imperialist strategies; but in those days, those countries had very little in the way of state welfare. During the twentieth century, all west European countries have in one way or another followed the German example by introducing various forms of tax-based provision for unemployment and sickness benefits, pensions, subsidized housing etc. How many of these countries have behaved aggressively?

In recent times, world opinion has criticized the USA for belligerence in Iraq and elsewhere, while European countries have often been considered too passive in the face of external threats. It is the Europeans who have extensive state welfare, of which America has relatively little.

However, it is belief in the universality of dogmas such as those of Mises, long current at the World Bank and the International Monetary Fund, that has led these institutions to try to impose modern American free-market orthodoxy indiscriminately on very different countries all over the world. The results of this inflexible policy have turned out to be deeply disappointing and have been widely criticized.

7

HAYEK,
APOSTLE OF NEGATIVE FREEDOM

The persistence of instinctual feelings of altruism and solidarity subjects those who follow the impersonal rules of the extended order [global free market] *to what is now fashionably called 'bad conscience'.*
FRIEDRICH VON HAYEK[1]

F riedrich von Hayek (1899–1992) was born in Vienna into a Catholic family steeped in academic and scientific culture. But he rejected the Christian faith at the age of eleven and remained all his life an atheist. As a young man he held somewhat socialist opinions, before his studies under Mises converted him to libertarianism. During the 1920s and 1930s, his observation of the tyrannies of Stalin and Hitler led him towards an obsession with the preservation of individual freedom.

HAYEK'S NEGATIVE FREEDOM

However, Hayek had no sympathy with the idea of freedom as it is understood in Catholic teaching. He considered that the only freedom that mattered was the *negative freedom* described by Isaiah Berlin (see Chapter 2). Hayek described this freedom as *the*

---

[1] Friedrich von Hayek, THE FATAL CONCEIT (London: Routledge, 1988), 64.

state in which a man is not subject to arbitrary coercion by the will of another or others.[2] Such coercion means, for Hayek, any situation where a person is *forced not to act according to a coherent plan of his own but to serve the ends of another.* Although Hayek uses the word *forced*, he does not mean physically compelled so that one has no choice. He means obliged to do something, the consequences of choosing not to do so being unacceptable.

Thus Hayek argued that the general in charge of an army or the director of a large construction project is less free than the poorest farmer or shepherd, since the general or the director *may have to change all his intentions and plans at a word from a superior.* Moreover, *the penniless vagabond ... is freer than the conscripted soldier*, while the *Jesuit who lives up to the ideals of the founder of his order* cannot be described as free, since he accepts total obedience to his superior. To be 'free', one must be in a position to live entirely according to one's own 'coherent plans' and in no way according to anyone else's wishes.

This conception of freedom is directly opposed to the Christian notion of submission of the individual will, as expressed by St Peter, *for the sake of the Lord, accept the authority of every human institution: the emperor, as the supreme authority, and the governors;*[3] or by Thomas à Kempis, *it is truly a great thing to live in obedience, to be under authority, and not to be our own masters.*[4]

---

[2] Hayek, THE CONSTITUTION OF LIBERTY (London: Routledge & Kegan Paul, 1960), 11 (Chapter 1). Other quotations in this and the following paragraph are from the same source.

[3] 1 PETER 2: 13 – 14.

[4] Thomas à Kempis, THE IMITATION OF CHRIST [*De Imitatione Christi*], Book I, Chap. 9 (my translation).

We must note that Hayekian freedom is not simply *absence of constraints* in general; it is absence of constraints imposed by the will of others. Impersonal constraints, according to Hayek, do not in any way encroach upon our freedom. Thus Hayek, a keen mountaineer, insists that the climber stuck in a crevasse *is not unfree* since he has not been deliberately confined by anyone else.[5]

ASSOCIATIONS DISAPPROVED

It is evident that, in Hayek's terms, any organization or association is, in principle, necessarily 'coercive', be it a business, an army, a ministry, a monastery, a family or even a couple. For no association can flourish if each of its members acts only on his or her own plans; there must be at least some coordination in pursuit of common goals.

Nevertheless, Hayek conceded that associations could be tolerated, on condition that membership in them be entirely voluntary. For him, any organization or association is in principle coercive, and thus destructive of its members' freedom, unless membership is strictly voluntary.

With explicit reference to families and to marriage, Hayek wrote that *society can do little to protect the individual* [from coercion] *beyond making such associations with others truly voluntary.*[6] But in relation to families, this desideratum is clearly absurd; one cannot choose voluntarily to be born into a particular family; and, from a Catholic standpoint, marriage (once contracted) can hardly be called a voluntary association.

---

[5] Hayek, THE CONSTITUTION OF LIBERTY, 12 – 13.
[6] Ibid., 138.

In general, it would seem that Hayekian freedom is attainable only in a society where there is little or no commitment among the management and staff of a company to stay together as a team; where there is little or no cohesion between members of a family; and where marriage is regarded as a contract terminable at will.

It is all too clear that Western societies have evolved more than a little towards such a situation, and this evolution owes a good deal to the influence of social and economic libertarians. All too many of us have what Aristotle called *a false idea of freedom*,[7] and the pursuit of this false freedom is pushing our societies towards grave instability or even anarchy.

And beyond that, perhaps, towards an authoritarianism that could follow such anarchy, such as we have already seen in Vladimir Putin's Russia, previously afflicted by an extreme and anarchic form of economic libertarianism.

REJECTION OF POSITIVE LAW

Hayek wrote extensively about the basic principles of law. He was fundamentally averse to law deliberately created by governments (*positive law*), as opposed to *natural law*, a system of fundamental principles of conduct that are deemed to apply naturally to all human beings at all times.

In Catholic terms, natural law is both known from nature by reason and seen as the revealed law of God, as expressed, for example, in the Ten Commandments. For Hayek, an atheist, natural law has to be 'discovered' by human reason; the task of the jurist is

---

[7] Aristotle, POLITICS. See Chapter 3, Note 13 supra.

not to create new laws but to discover, and apply, the basic general principles that constitute the underlying, unchanging law.

In practice, according to Hayek, the law of the land should consist essentially of the precedents created over the centuries by judges as they decide cases in accordance with the principles of natural law. In making these decisions, judges should take great care to respect existing precedents (their predecessors' decisions) and to deviate therefrom as little as possible.

This would, of course, be a rigid, inflexible, impersonal legal system, but Hayek wanted it that way because of his belief that impersonal constraints do not reduce our freedom. If judges were allowed to exercise their own discretion by interpreting laws in the light of historical development, or of the particular circumstances of the case being heard, then litigating parties, or accused persons, would be subject to constraint by the personal decisions of judges; they would lose their 'freedom'.

The Hayekian legal system would thus be highly conservative, in the original and literal sense of that word. It could only develop, change and adapt very slowly. One has to wonder how such a system could possibly keep pace with the fully liberalized Hayekian economy and society, where fierce competition in deregulated markets encourages very rapid innovation and change.

Hayek's concept of the law reflects his desire that society should be governed by impersonal mechanisms, which do not impinge upon personal freedom, rather than by collective or state decisions, said to of personal origin, and therefore destructive of freedom. Thus, Hayek deplored the tendency of modern governments to constantly legislate. He looked back nostalgically to medieval Europe, where, he tells us:

> *Law was ... regarded as something given independently of human will, something to be discovered, not made, and ... the conception that law could be deliberately made or altered seemed almost sacrilegious.*[8]

We see here the basis of Hayek's anti-statist doctrine. He demanded a minimum state which would refrain strictly from expressing any kind of collective will. Thus,

> *Common concrete ends are replaced by common abstract rules. Government is needed only to enforce these abstract rules, and thereby to protect the individual against coercion, or invasion of his free sphere, by others. Whereas enforced obedience to common concrete ends is tantamount to slavery, obedience to common abstract rules (however burdensome they may still feel) provides scope for the most extraordinary freedom and diversity.*[9]

So confident was he in the possibility that society could be 'flown on auto-pilot' by impersonal mechanisms – the free market and the unchanging common law – that he made a truly astounding claim: he maintained that his ideal individualist polity was *a social system which does not depend for its functioning on our finding good men for running it.*[10] (And he did not mean that society should be run by good women!)

Hayek considered all political power to be intrinsically bad: *to the great individualist social philosophers of the nineteenth century ...*

---

[8] Hayek, Law, Legislation and Liberty, Vol. I (Chicago: University Press, 1973), 83.

[9] Hayek, The Fatal Conceit, 63.

[10] Hayek, Individualism and Economic Order (Chicago: University Press, 1948), 12.

power itself has always appeared the arch-evil.[11] One might as well say that electricity is evil, because it is dangerous unless it is properly insulated and controlled. This attitude denies even the possibility of cultivating the art of good government. Should we be surprised to find that certain countries, governed by political parties which have perversely adopted the ideology of contempt for the state, are badly governed?

RULE OF THE MARKET

Here we encounter one of the two main pillars of the Hayekian idolatry of the free market. For the market, like the common law, is deemed to be an impersonal mechanism which cannot damage individual freedom. But this is so, he claimed, only if the market is truly free, unconstrained by decisions made by politicians, trade or professional associations, trade unions or other bodies which may express and impose personal influence.

Let us note an interesting consequence of Hayek's bizarre logic. In the early nineteenth century, the completely unregulated labor market made English textile workers toil for thirteen or fourteen hours a day. Lord Shaftesbury's legislation, the *Factory Act* (also called the *Ten Hour Act*) of 1847 limited the working day (originally only for women and children) to ten hours.

So, according to Hayek's theory, before 1847 the textile workers were free, since they were forced to work excessive hours only by the impersonal dictates of the market.[12] After Shaftesbury's leg-

---

[11] Hayek, THE ROAD TO SERFDOM (London: Routledge & Kegan Paul, 1944), 107.
[12] One might argue that they were forced by their employers rather than 'by the market'. But the employers themselves, in the absence of regulation, acted under compelling market pressures.

islation, however, they lost their freedom, because their working hours were thenceforth determined by political will, not by the impersonal market.

Following the same logic, trade unionism is fundamentally unacceptable. A union member is subject to collective agreements negotiated by his or her union. This, according to Hayek, is a denial of freedom, since a trade union is not an impersonal force; its agreements reflect the personal wills of the negotiators on both sides. To remain free, the worker ought rather to make his or her own individual contract with the employer.

What is the other pillar of the aforesaid market idolatry? It is the theory of *distributed intelligence*. This begins with the correct observation that the 'market' (that is, the market as a whole, the aggregate of all the various particular markets in the entire economy) possesses in effect a synthesis of innumerable economic facts.

The market 'knows' the current demand of every buyer, at any moment, for each product and service available in the whole economy, as well as the current offering of every seller, at any moment, of all those products and services. As Hayek observes,

> *The shipper who earns his living from using otherwise empty or half-filled journeys of tramp-steamers, or the estate agent whose whole knowledge is almost exclusively one of temporary opportunities … perform eminently useful functions based on special knowledge of circumstances of the fleeting moment not known to others.*[13]

The argument continues: to centralize all that knowledge in a planning organization, and to keep it up to date, would clearly be

---

[13] Hayek, INDIVIDUALISM AND ECONOMIC ORDER, 80.

impossible. It follows that, as an efficient determinant of the correct prices of goods and services, and the quantities thereof to be supplied, the market is far superior to any kind of central planning.

Therefore, say the free-marketeers, all such planning is pointless. It is far better to leave everything to the omniscient untrammeled market, which creates its own *spontaneous order.*

MARKET IS KNOWLEDGEABLE,
YET IGNORANT

Now this theory looks highly plausible; but it is also questionable. For it is a curious fact that, although the market is extraordinarily 'knowledgeable', it can behave as though it is deeply ignorant. Thus, the market behaves as if it does not know that it is necessary for us to limit our consumption of petroleum products, firstly because we have a duty to conserve supplies for future generations, secondly because excessive consumption of these products is dangerously degrading our climate.

Again, the market sometimes behaves as if it does not know that a worker requires a living wage; the wage level arising in a free labor market can, in some circumstances, be less than enough to live on. Menger (Chapter 5) admitted that this actually happened, and Mises (Chapter 6) admitted that it was possible.

One may reply, sure enough, that the individuals who participate in the market do, of course, know these facts. But, in practice, they tend to behave in the market as if they did not know. And though this behavior is perverse, there are logical and practical reasons for it. If you are running a transport company, you cannot replace diesel fuel with much more expensive liquid hydrogen while your competitors are not doing likewise; you would very soon be run out of business. If you are trading in a sector where current wages are barely enough to live on, you cannot pay your workers much more than the norm so long as you are up against competitors who do not share your scruples.

In fact, therefore, strange as it may seem, the market 'does not know', or acts as if it did not know, realities that are well known to its participants. That is why interference with the market, either by the state or by agreement between competing participants, may be necessary.

Nevertheless, devotees of Hayekian economics persist in believing that we are entitled, even morally obliged, always to follow without hesitation the sacrosanct *price signals* given by the free market, since the market, they say, possesses an omniscience that is beyond the reach of individuals, governments or planning offices.

Let us not be intimidated by these pretentious dogmatists. The paradoxical truth is that *markets are extremely knowledgeable, but also gravely ignorant.*

NO MEANING FOR SOCIAL JUSTICE

If one accepts that impersonal forces cannot encroach on our freedom, it follows that the operations of the free market, being considered impersonal, cannot damage individual freedom. Moreover, Hayek argues that the impersonal free market does not damage *either freedom or justice*. Its consequences cannot be described as unjust (or, for that matter, just).

Thus, those who find themselves sunk in penury or unemployment, as a consequence of the caprices of the market, do not lack freedom; nor do they lack justice. For the market is like a game in which *there is no sense in calling the outcome either just or unjust.*[14]

Hayek insists that *'social justice' is an empty phrase with no determinable meaning.*[15] He complains that *the Roman Catholic Church in particular has made the goal of social justice part of its official doctrine.*[16] Further, Hayek rejects entirely the principle of *distributive justice*, arguing that

> *The results of the individual's efforts are necessarily unpredictable, and the question of whether the resulting distribution of incomes is just or unjust has no meaning.*[17]

According to this thesis, it is inadmissible to correct excessive inequalities via the tax system, since taxing citizens at different rates violates the principle of equality before the law.

In effect, Hayek was opposed to practically all efforts by government to reduce poverty, since he believed that such efforts endangered citizens' freedom. Nevertheless, he did grudgingly tolerate

> ... *some provision for those threatened by the extremes of indigence or starvation, be it only in the interest of those who require protection against acts of desperation on the part of the needy.*[18]

---

[14] Hayek, THE MIRAGE OF SOCIAL JUSTICE, Vol. II of LAW, LEGISLATION AND LIBERTY (Chicago: University Press, 1976), 126.

[15] Ibid., 133.

[16] Ibid., 66.

[17] Hayek, THE CONSTITUTION OF LIBERTY, 99.

[18] Ibid., 285.

Contempt for solidarity, and for social or communal altruism, is fundamental in Hayek's philosophy. He detested the practice of solidarity, particularly by trade unions, firstly because this interferes with the freedom of action of individuals, as we have explained; secondly, because if solidarity in the workplace does protect the interests of workers, this must be detrimental to consumers.

A plant or industry cannot be conducted in the interest of some permanent distinct body of workers if it is at the same time to serve the interest of the consumers.[19]

As is normal with libertarian economists, Hayek assumed that the interest of the consumers should take absolute precedence over that of the workers.

Trade unions, in Hayek's view, are in any case useless, even counterproductive. *They are the prime source of unemployment,*[20] he thunders, because if they do indeed succeed in improving members' wages, then they must necessarily reduce the numbers of workers employed, and/or the wages of non-members.

The possibility that workers as a class might improve their share in the total revenue of the economy is not admitted.

However, it is well known that the workers' share in total American incomes (and likewise in other countries) has diminished in recent years, to the benefit of shareholders and overpaid top executives.

If the workers' share can fall, it can also rise. But for that to happen, the workers need to unite to protect their interests.

---

[19] Ibid., 277.
[20] Hayek, UNEMPLOYMENT AND THE UNIONS (London: Institute of Economic Affairs, 1980), 52.

Why reject, as Hayek clearly does, the concept of *altruism*, except within the narrow circle of family and close friends? Because altruism in regard to society at large – the unselfish pursuit of the public interest or common good – implies a vision of what is good for society, for the community as a whole.

That is precisely what libertarians abhor. Firstly, because, as we have seen in our discussion of *distributed intelligence*, they think that individuals or governments cannot know what is good for society as a whole. Or, at least, they cannot know nearly as well as the market knows. Secondly, because libertarians fear that we may lose our freedom by making ourselves follow a prearranged plan for the common good, rather than 'acting according to coherent plans of our own'..

We are thus driven back to that favorite libertarian maxim, that we can only do good to the community by blindly pursuing our own personal interests. In his last book, THE FATAL CONCEIT, Hayek went so far as to say that we should *gain from* not *treating one another as neighbors*.[21] The ugliness of this notion surely indicates that there underlies it a fundamental error.

---

[21] Hayek, THE FATAL CONCEIT, 13.

8

ROTHBARD

THE ANARCHO-CAPITALIST

*In Rothbard's hands, Misesian orthodoxy took the
form of a 'gospel', passing from the defense of the market to redemption by the market.*
GILLES CAMPAGNOLO[1]

M urray Rothbard (1926-1995), though American by birth
and residence, is considered a member of the Austrian
school, since he was a pupil and admirer of Mises, about whose
ideas he wrote extensively. He regarded Mises' book HUMAN AC-
TION as *one of the finest products of the human mind in our century.*[2]
Rothbard is indeed considered in America as the most successful
popularizer of Mises.

But he not only followed the latter's teachings; he extended
them a good deal further. He developed an *anarcho-capitalist* philosophy, distinct from that of Mises, who never accepted anar-

---

[1] Gilles Campagnolo, SEULS LES EXTRÉMISTES SONT COHÉRENTS (Lyon: ENS Editions,
2006), 133. The title of this book translates a characteristic remark by Rothbard, *only
extremists make sense*. The author is a researcher at the Centre National de la Re-
cherche Scientifique in France.
[2] Murray N. Rothbard, LUDWIG VON MISES: SCHOLAR, CREATOR, HERO (Auburn,
Alabama: Ludwig von Mises Institute, 1988), 51.

chism. For Rothbard, *capitalism is the fullest expression of anarchism, and anarchism is the fullest expression of capitalism.*[3]

CRITIQUE OF OTHER ECONOMISTS

Rothbard was highly critical of the economists of the neoclassical school, such as Milton Friedman and Kenneth Arrow in the USA, Gérard Debreu in France, for he considered that their methods, based on mathematical modeling, were unrealistic. He blamed them for

> ... *a plague of modeling, complaining that people do not construct theories any more; they 'build' models of the society or economy. Yet no-one seems to notice the peculiar inaptness of the concept.*[4]

In the same essay he ridicules the so-called *Wertfreiheit* (freedom from value judgments) of certain economists:

> *The current fashion is to preserve a façade of Wertfreiheit, while casually adopting value judgments, not as the scientist's (economist's) own decision, but as the consensus of the values of others.*[5]

Even a non-admirer of Rothbard may well feel a certain sympathy with him on this matter.

In an extraordinary diatribe entitled "The Celebrated Adam Smith," Rothbard asserts that Smith *originated nothing that was true, and whatever he originated was wrong.* He complains that THE WEALTH OF NATIONS, Smith's economic masterpiece,

---

[3] Interview in THE NEW BANNER, 25 February 1972. This interview is accessible on *www.mises.org/web/2667* (accessed 1 July 2010).

[4] Rothbard, "The Mantle of Science," SCIENTISM AND VALUE, ed. Helmut Schoeck and James Wiggins (Princeton, New Jersey: Van Nostrand, 1960), 159-180.

[5] Ibid.

was somehow able to blind all men to the very knowledge that other economists, let alone better ones, had existed and written before 1776.[6]

As we shall see, Rothbard held that the foundations of the true economic faith had been laid by certain late medieval Spanish theologians, but were then built over and hidden by the reactionary thinkers of the British Enlightenment. Smith was wrong, according to Rothbard, because he adopted a cost-of-production theory of value, rather than the true subjective theory later advanced by Menger; because he did not favor strict adherence to the gold standard; because he did not venerate entrepreneurs; because he believed in

> *... the unfortunate fallacy that wages ... are determined by the 'bargaining power' of employers and workers. It was a simple leap from that position to the pro-union propagandists claiming erroneously that unions can raise overall wage rates throughout the economy.*[7]

Worst of all,

> *... in The Wealth of Nations ... laissez-faire becomes only a qualified presumption rather than a hard-and-fast rule, and the natural order becomes imperfect and to be followed only 'in most cases'... indeed, the list of exceptions Smith makes to laissez-faire is surprisingly long.*[8]

Very few economists were sufficiently hard-and-fast to please Rothbard.

---

[6] Rothbard, "The Celebrated Adam Smith," AN AUSTRIAN PERSPECTIVE ON THE HISTORY OF ECONOMIC THOUGHT (London: Edward Elgar, 1995), Vol. I, Chap. 16, 435-6.
[7] Rothbard, AN AUSTRIAN PERSPECTIVE, 459.
[8] Ibid., 465. See, for example, THE WEALTH OF NATIONS, Book 4, Chap. 2.

In one of his major works, AN AUSTRIAN PERSPECTIVE ON THE HISTORY OF ECONOMIC THOUGHT, Rothbard claims that modern economics originated not with the Enlightenment thinkers (Quesnay, Turgot, Smith, Ricardo and others, i.e. the *classical school* of economics); but rather with the *School of Salamanca*, a group of scholastic theologians that included Luis Molina SJ (1535-1600), Francisco Suárez SJ (1548-1617) and Domingo de Soto OP (1494-1560), all based at the University of Salamanca.[9]

This claim is controversial, as some consider Rothbard's view to be a misreading of the Salamanca scholars.

Others argue that the first scholastic to express 'proto-libertarian' views was Juan de Mariana SJ (1536-1624), who was not a member of the Salamanca school. Mariana was a critic of excessive state spending, inflationary taxation and state intervention in economic matters.

Not surprisingly, neoconservative Catholics love the idea that Salamanca (and perhaps even St Thomas) equated *justum pretium* (just price) with the current market price.

If this could be substantiated, it would provide significant support for their claim that, despite what the Vatican says today, libertarian economics has its roots in the thoughts of certain Catholic scholastic theologians.

However, given that free-market prices tend to vary widely, rapidly and erratically, it is somewhat difficult to see how the market price can provide a standard for interpretation of Thomas's

---

[9] Ibid., Chap. 4, passim.

rule, *it is unjust and unlawful to sell anything for more than it is worth, or buy for less than it is worth.* [10] Thomas seems to have desired a certain stability, than which few things are more hateful to libertarians.

Rothbard, of Jewish origin, was a lifelong agnostic. However, he took a keen interest in religious influences on economic thought. He argued that the 'liturgical' churches (Catholic, Anglican, Lutheran) were traditionally favorable to the free market, while Reformed and Evangelical churches were more inclined towards communitarianism and socialism. [11]

In particular, he felt that Adam Smith's 'errors' were rooted in his Calvinist (Presbyterian) background. However, according to Rothbard, these tendencies *inverted* during the last decades of the twentieth century, the Catholic and other liturgical churches moving to the left, and the Evangelicals to the right.

The notion that Catholic teaching tended to favor libertarian economics until the second half of the twentieth century is debatable, however, given the vigorous development of Catholic social teaching ever since RERUM NOVARUM, which, though anti-socialist, explicitly favors the development of labor unions and countenances state regulation of working conditions where necessary. [12] And indeed the development of modern Catholic thought on economic matters can be traced back well beyond RERUM NOVARUM, as we shall see in Chapter 10.

---

[10] St Thomas Aquinas, SUMMA THEOLOGICA, Secunda Secundae, Q. 77, Art. 1.
[11] Harry C. Veryser, "Murray Rothbard in Memoriam," THE INTERCOLLEGIATE REVIEW (Wilmington, Delaware, Fall 1995), 41.
[12] Pope Leo XIII, encyclical RERUM NOVARUM (1891), Par. 45.

Rothbard's anarchistic opinions are based on a so-called principle of natural law, namely (in Rothbard's words) the *non-aggression axiom*, that is to say: *no man or group of men may aggress against the person or property of anyone else.*[13] The word *aggression* is defined thus:

> ... *the initiation or use or threat of physical violence against the person or property of someone else ... if no man may aggress against ... the person or property of another, this means that every man is free to do whatever he wishes, except commit such aggression.*[14]

Rules laid down by governments qualify as 'aggression' because they are enforceable, in the last resort, by 'physical violence' (arrest and imprisonment). One notes the resemblance to Hayek's definition of negative liberty.

Rothbard's principle of non-aggression is reminiscent of John Stuart Mill's *harm principle*, namely that, as an individual, one is entitled to do as one likes so long as one does not harm others. As Mill puts it,

> *The only purpose for which power can be rightfully exercised over any member of a civilized community, against his will, is to prevent harm to others. His own good, either physical or moral, is not a sufficient warrant.*[15]

---

[13] Rothbard, FOR A NEW LIBERTY, second edition (Auburn, Alabama: Ludwig von Mises Institute, 2006), 27.

[14] Ibid.

[15] John Stuart Mill, ON LIBERTY (1869) (New York: Liberal Arts Press, 1956), Chap. I, 13.

This view is somewhat difficult to justify; for, in harming one-self, one is very likely to harm others, as for example the person who indulges in drug or alcohol abuse usually causes trouble to his or her family, friends or colleagues. Even in cases where the harm to others is less obvious, it is probable that the effects of self-damaging behavior are not free from 'collateral damage' to other people. Thus Fr. Frederick Copleston SJ observed that:

> Mill quotes[16] with approval Wilhelm von Humboldt's statement that the end of man is 'the highest and most harmonious development of his powers to a complete and consistent whole'. And Mill is, of course, convinced that the common happiness of man is increased if individuals do develop themselves in this way. Might it not be argued, therefore, that harm is done to others, to the community, if the individual acts in such a way as to prevent the harmonious integration of his powers and becomes a warped personality?[17]

Ideally, everyone should make some positive contribution to the good of human society. Those who damage themselves may become unable to do so, and may indeed contribute more harm than good to society.

HOSTILITY TO GOVERNMENT

The attitudes of libertarians such as Mill and Rothbard mean in effect that the state has no right to try to encourage or enforce any moral standards. It is entitled only to restrain people from positively injuring one another; on no account to attack the roots of

---

[16] Ibid., Chap. III, 69.
[17] Frederick Copleston, HISTORY OF PHILOSOPHY, Vol. VIII, (London: Burns & Oates, 1966), 137.

the problem, namely the kinds of faulty morality that lead to injurious behavior. Rothbard continues:

> *The libertarian favors the right to unrestricted private property and free-exchange; hence, a system of 'laissez-faire capitalism' ... only libertarians are prepared to call taxation what it is: legalized and organized theft on a grand scale ... whatever services the government actually performs could be supplied far more efficiently and far more morally by private or cooperative enterprise.*[18]

According to Rothbard, even governmental functions such as the police, the courts and the armed forces could and should be privatized. He totally rejects the idea that the state is capable of being a beneficent agent. He continues:

> *If you wish to know how libertarians regard the state ... simply think of the state as a criminal band, and all of the libertarian attitudes will logically fall into place.*[19]

This is a deplorably negative attitude. It is true that we may on occasion make the mistake of electing criminals to govern us; but surely it is possible to do better.

Rothbard argues that pornography, sexual deviations and prostitution must be tolerated:

> *The good, bad or indifferent consequences of pornography ... are completely irrelevant to the question of whether or not it should be outlawed. The libertarian holds that it is not the business of the law ... to enforce anyone's concept of morality.*[20]

---

[18] Rothbard, FOR A NEW LIBERTY, 28-30.
[19] Ibid., 57.
[20] Ibid., 127.

He looks back nostalgically to the days before brothels were out-lawed in most American states, lamenting the disappearance of houses

> *operated by madams anxious to cultivate goodwill among cus-tomers over a long time span … competing to provide high-quality service and build up a 'brand name'.*[21]

In addition, he claims that abortion must be tolerated, but not because of any Jewish doctrine concerning the status of the fetus. No, Rothbard's curious argument is that

> *no being has a right to live, unbidden, as a parasite within or upon some person's body* [since such a right would contra-vene] *the absolute right of every person, and hence every wom-an, to the ownership of her own body.*[22]

From the principle that no person must be constrained to do, or not to do, anything, it follows that no human authority is legi-timate. Even the prevention of aggression could be left to private-enterprise armed forces and to prosecution of aggressors in pri-vate-sector courts. Therefore, society does not have the right to establish a state of any kind whatever. Anarchy rules! And, accord-ing to Rothbard, this principle is imposed by natural law.

NATURAL LAW WITHOUT AUTHORITY?

Now, since Aristotle and Cicero, philosophers and theologians and jurists have never ceased to concern themselves with natural law. It is the corpus of fundamental laws that are considered to

---

[21] Ibid., 130. Rothbard, born in 1926, presumably did not write this from personal experience, since brothels had been outlawed in almost all states since the period 1910-1915.
[22] Ibid., 132.

exist 'naturally', to have been enacted by 'nature' and not by us, and thus to apply to all humanity, at all times and in all places.

According to St Thomas, natural law is our participation in the divine law; that part of the divine law that is revealed to us by *natural reason*.[23] Over the centuries, those who have studied the question of natural law have certainly not generally thought that it rules out human authority.

How then did Rothbard come to differentiate himself from practically all his predecessors? According to Rothbard, reason leads us to think that natural law does not in any way admit the exercise by one person of authority over another. For we are necessarily 'all equal before natural law'; but authority of one person over another implies inequality, whereof Rothbard gives as an example, *the view that Hohenzollerns are by nature entitled to rule over non-Hohenzollerns*.[24]

It follows that one could admit the principle of authority only on condition that each person held authority over all others in equal shares. Thus, if there were, for example, only a hundred human beings in existence, then each could be subject equally to the authority of the other ninety-nine; thus each could so nothing without the permission of the other ninety-nine. Which is evidently absurd. Moreover, by extension, in the real world, each one of us would be subject, in equal parts, to the authority of the 6.8 billion other human beings! According to Rothbard, this fine example of *reductio ad absurdum* demonstrates that all authority is unacceptable.

---

[23] St Thomas Aquinas, SUMMA THEOLOGICA, Prima Secundae, Q. 91.
[24] Rothbard, THE ETHICS OF LIBERTY (1982) (New York: University Press, 1998), 45.

Clearly, neither Jewish nor Christian doctrine agrees. Scripture endorses the necessity of human authority, while insisting that such authority is granted by God to rulers and must be exercised in accordance with God's will.[25]

St Thomas argued that human beings *even in the state of innocence* would have been unequal simply by virtue of being different and not identical; therefore it would still have been appropriate for those having the skill to rule to do so.[26]

The eighteenth-century English anarchist William Godwin contrived to circumvent this argument by postulating that we are all born the same; our differences are not innate but circumstantial:

> *The characters of men originate in their external circumstances … the actions and dispositions of men are not the offspring of any original bias that they bring into the world … they are the offspring of circumstances and events.*[27]

But that is, to say the least, difficult to believe.

AGAINST GOVERNMENT SOCIAL PROGRAMS

In condemning all forms of taxation, Rothbard clearly rejects, as did Mises, all attempts by the state to reduce inequalities. This issue distances the Austrian economists from the neoclassicals, some of whom accept in principle the possibility of levying a once-for-all tax (such as an inheritance tax) on large fortunes and transferring the product thereof to the poor.

---

[25] See, for example, CATECHISM OF THE CATHOLIC CHURCH, op. cit. supra, Pars. 1897 ff.

[26] St Thomas Aquinas, SUMMA THEOLOGICA, Prima, Q. 96.

[27] William Godwin, POLITICAL JUSTICE (1798), Book I, Chap. 4, ed. F. E. L. Priestly (facsimile, Toronto: University Press, 1946), 24 – 27.

For Rothbard, such a practice would be out of the question. He admits that people sometimes ask,

what is the justification for someone whose only merit is being born a Rockefeller inheriting far more wealth than someone born a Rothbard?[28]

He cunningly avoids answering this question: *the libertarian answer is to concentrate* not *on the recipient ... but on the* giver, *the man who bestows the inheritance,*[29] who is entitled to dispose of his fortune as he pleases.

However, though Rothbard rejects utterly any form of state welfare benefits, he goes out of his way to extol the system of poverty relief run by the Latter-Day Saints (Mormons).

The Mormon Church operates an extensive private welfare plan for its members ... there is no finer model than the Mormon Church for a private, voluntary, rational, individualistic welfare program.[30]

This passes the Rothbard test because it is said to be 'voluntary', unlike tax-based state systems. Mormons are expected to pay tithes (10%) of their income to finance this system. Let us turn to a well-researched text on Mormonism to discover what this means in practice.

People called to assignments [to serve the church in various ways] *are expected to be 'worthy' – a word which in the Mormon vocabulary means that one pays tithes and offerings ... only those worthy of 'recommends'* [certificates of worthiness from their bishops] *may enter the temple ... at the end of*

---

[28] Rothbard, FOR A NEW LIBERTY, 49.
[29] Ibid., 49.
[30] Ibid., 183 & 186.

every year the bishop of the ward holds a 'tithing settlement'; family members are expected to meet with their bishop and discuss their particular situation, ideally reporting that they have paid a 'full tithe' for the year.[31]

Libertarians insist that any transfers from rich to poor must be 'voluntary'; but it would seem that Mormon tithes, like the *tzedakah* of Jewish tradition, are in fact more obligatory than voluntary. And why not? If contributions were truly voluntary, some would not pay; then either the others would have to pay more than their fair share, or the benefits would be inadequate.

What, then, are we to make of the bizarre philosophy of Rothbard? Should we take it seriously? If that means accepting it as moral, realistic and practical, the answer must surely be no. Nevertheless, Rothbard does provide a useful illustration of what happens when Austrian principles are taken to their logical conclusions.

Mises, for example, denied that he was an anarchist. But he argued (see Chapter 6) that *no-one has the right to substitute his own value judgments for those of the acting individual*; this attitude implies the Rothbardian view that the law has no business imposing upon any individual the moral concepts of the legislators. Likewise Mises' anti-statism and insistence on *laissez-faire* as the only acceptable economic way are but somewhat milder versions of Rothbard's positions.

It is not difficult to see the influence of Rothbard in the perverse, dangerous, but currently fashionable ideas promoted in the

---

[31] L.J. Arrington & D. Bitton, THE MORMON EXPERIENCE (New York: Knopf, 1979), 293-300.

United States by the Tea Party movement. To argue successfully against such tendencies, we need to have some familiarity with their underlying ideology, so that we can understand and explain where and how they have gone wrong.

9

CONSEQUENCES OF

LIBERTARIANISM

We've made a virtue of competition,
which means other people are a threat, not a support.
RICHARD LAYARD[1]

THE BANKING CRISIS

T he crisis of 2008/09 began in the banking sector which, particularly in the USA, had become increasingly overblown and unstable in recent years. The growth of a huge 'bubble' of excessive, unsound lending and speculative trading was the outcome of the worldwide tendency, traceable to the 1970s, to deregulate the financial system, in the belief that by allowing businesses more 'negative freedom' (absence of constraints) we would have more dynamic, efficient, prosperous economies.

There is a deeper underlying reason for the institutional changes of the past forty years. Regulation means that businesses are subject to *ad hoc* rules laid down by governments and regula-

---

[1] Quoted by Catherine Mayer in TIME MAGAZINE, 7 April 2008, 44. Layard is a professor at the London School of Economics.

tors, rather than (as Austrians wish) simply to basic general legal principles and to the impersonal 'laws' of the free market, such as: business goes to the firm that makes the best price. According to Hayek, *ad hoc* regulation is objectionable because it destroys 'freedom', as he defined it. Austrian influence has thus provided the ideological basis for a long-term trend towards discarding traditional regulations.

Moreover, Austrian theory rejects limitations on competition, partly because these restrict commercial 'freedom', and partly because, as Menger explained, untrammeled competition encourages maximum production of everything. In today's banking world, this means maximum lending and maximum trading in financial instruments.

Competition encourages the development of increasingly complex investments, as each bank seeks to gain competitive advantage by offering something new and different. Hence the proliferation of unfamiliar bonds and derivative contracts of excessive complexity, and thus of uncertain value. Here lies one cause of the breakdown in confidence in financial markets. If a bank holds large quantities of investments which are innovative, intricate, poorly understood 'products', whose value in abnormal times is highly uncertain, then confidence in the bank is enfeebled. And banking relies totally on confidence.

The deregulation of American banking included a bonfire of restrictions on the geographical location and permitted activities of financial concerns. Until the 1980s, no American bank was allowed to have branches in more than one state; this limitation has largely disappeared. There was also, traditionally, a clear division of functions between commercial banks and 'thrifts'. Banks offered business and consumer loans and money transmission services; thrifts (savings and loans institutions, mutual savings banks), provided savings accounts and house-purchase loans.

Again, this distinction has largely broken down. Most of the mutual savings banks, like their British equivalents (*building societies*), have 'demutualized'; they are now companies with shareholders, more concerned with maximizing profits than were the old-style mutuals. The 'Glass-Steagall' division between commercial banks and investment banks, which were less strictly regulated because they did not accept deposits from the general public, has gone the way of other constraints.[2] There were also limits on the rates of interest paid on deposits, and on the amount that could be lent on mortgage (percentage of the value of the property mortgaged). These limits have gone too.

The object of all this deregulation has been to bring financial services into line with the ideology of maximum commercial freedom, and to enhance competition. All this might have been good in moderation, but it has gone much too far. Over-competitive lending activity in the mortgage market has brought us the infamous profusion of dubious subprime mortgages, whose failures triggered off the present crisis. So much for those free-market economists who argue that *competition is always good*.[3]

---

[2] "Glass-Steagall" is the name given to the U.S. Banking Act of 1933 which established this division. It was named after two senators of the Democratic Party who introduced the legislation. The Act was repealed in 1999 by the Gramm-Leach-Bliley Act, named after the Republican Party senators who introduced it.

[3] Pascal Salin (Université Paris Dauphine), "Il faut sauver le soldat Bolkestein!" in LE FIGARO (Paris) 2 February 2005.

American banking history is a story of continuous tension between bankers, seeking freedom to do as they please, and regulators, seeking a stable financial environment. For forty years or so after 1929, the regulators were on top; for the next forty, the bankers were on top. Time now for a reversal!

UNEMPLOYMENT

For many years after the depression of the 1930s, rates of unemployment were generally low in the developed countries. The introduction of 'Austrian' economic policies from the 1970s onwards was followed by a period of generally much higher rates which continues to this day. Are there clear causal links? I think there are.

Austrianism, as we have seen, essentially treats labor simply as a tool needed in production; it is unconcerned with pursuing the best interests of the workers as a primary objective. This follows from Mises' insistence that *labor is a means, not an end in itself.*[4] As Yamawaki observes,

> *Neoliberals, who emphasized the importance of efficiency, paid little attention to the circumstances of workers and even regarded the trade union as unnecessary.*[5]

The term *neoliberals* includes both neoclassicals and Austrians. Their obsession with efficiency translates, on the shop floor, into ever-rising *labor productivity*, i.e. achieving a given level of production with minimum input of labor. In order to maximize productivity, neoliberals insist on untrammeled competition, which moti-

---

[4] See Chapter 6, note 16.
[5] See Chapter 4, note 35.

vates, indeed compels, businesses to reduce their labor costs whe-rever possible. Is it surprising that such economic policies tend to increase unemployment?

Austrian economists reply that their policies benefit the work-ers indirectly. Thus, for example, rising productivity in the auto industry means less employment therein, but it also means that cars become cheaper. Those who buy cars therefore have more cash available to spend, for example, on eating out, thus stimulat-ing restaurant employment. The workers no longer employed in Detroit can find work at McDonalds; so they are still employed, and they can buy cars more cheaply. In the end, so the theory tells us, they are better off.

The theory does not work so well in practice. For one thing, McDonalds pays a good deal less than is (or was) usual in the De-troit auto works, partly because auto workers have generally had strong unions; these (at least in the USA) are not recognized, or even tolerated, under the golden arches.

More generally, the problem with the relentless pursuit of productivity is that employment in new or expanding businesses may not grow fast enough to offset cutbacks in established firms which are replacing workers with machinery. Why not stimulate sufficient general economic growth to overcome this problem? Because this may be inflationary; and in the background is the worry that rapid growth may wreak yet more damage on our en-vironment.

The current worldwide obsession with increasing labor prod-uctivity, stimulated and imposed by global competition, has created a situation of increasingly rapid economic change; a world where jobs are increasingly hard to find and hard to keep.

One is reminded of an experiment at the *Gare Montparnassse* in Paris a few years ago. This is a big railway station with complex links to the *Métro* (city subway); one of these links involves a lengthy ride on a moving walkway. This machine was accelerated to run at 11 kilometers per hour (almost 7 miles per hour); but the experiment failed. Too many passengers lost their balance and fell down when joining or leaving the high-speed 'rolling carpet' (*tapis roulant*). There were some serious accidents, and the speed has had to be cut back.

Likewise the 'dynamic economy' of rapid, indeed accelerating, change, adored by the free-marketeers, is a machine which trips too many people up and leaves them injured. Economies today are changing at a pace that, historically speaking, is abnormal or even unprecedented. As a result, there are too many casualties. The customary response is that this is something we must accept, since we cannot avoid it.

It does not seem to occur to the proponents of this view that excessively rapid change is a consequence of economic policies which we have chosen quite deliberately to follow, namely deregulation and the promotion of maximum competition.

WORKING CONDITIONS

Austrian economics tends to follow Mises' assumption that *labor is the most scarce of all the primary means of production.*[6] This implies that workers are normally in a strong bargaining position vis-

[6] See Chapter 6, note 19.

à-vis employers; so they do not need strong unions or protective legislation restricting hours of work, prescribing minimum rates of pay and so on.

In reality, as we have noted, there is nowadays little or no truth in Mises' assumption. Energy and materials are becoming increasingly scarce and costly, while there are also constraints on our use of resources; we need to curb our use of fossil fuels to reduce emissions of greenhouse gases; we need to cut down fewer trees (or plant more), because the shrinkage of forests is another factor aggravating the carbon problem. Labor is no longer the scarcest resource, if it ever was.

But faith in Mises' ideas has supported policies that weaken both the unions and the legal framework of worker protection.

These policies, combined with others that favor harsher competition, have had unsurprising consequences: our conditions of work have in general deteriorated. Jobs are less secure; in many countries, pay has not risen in line with GDP; hours of work have often lengthened; work tends to be more stressful.

In 2007 the European Agency for Health and Safety at Work published a report in which we find the following observations:[7]

- *Over recent decades, significant changes in the world of work have led … to new and increasing psycho-social risks.*

- *The major problems appear to be: precarious and insecure employment, the ageing workforce, work intensification, violence and bullying at the workplace, and poor work-life balance.*

---

[7] Report : EXPERT FORECAST ON EMERGING PSYCHOSOCIAL RISKS RELATED TO OCCUPATIONAL SAFETY AND HEALTH, 24; see
http://osha.europa.eu/en/publications/reports/7807118/view. (Accessed 1 July 2010).

- *Among the main symptoms observed are: exhaustion or 'bur-nout', depression, muscular pains, hypertension, insomnia, loss of appetite, loss of memory, even paranoid disorders and suicide.*

INEQUALITY

It is clear that inequalities have considerably increased over the past thirty to forty years in most developed countries. Concerning the USA, the French economist Thomas Piketty has observed that, over two decades (the 1980s and 1990s), *American inequalities seem to have reverted to the level they stood at just before the First World War.*[8]

How is this trend linked with Austrian economics? One link is the Austrian argument that any attempt to mitigate inequalities would damage the functioning of the market system. Mises, for example, wrote that

> *inequality of income and capital is an inherent characteristic of market economies. Its elimination would entirely destroy the market economy.*[9]

He believed that entrepreneurs must be allowed to expand their businesses without limit under their personal ownership:

> *A law that prohibits any individual from accumulating more than ten millions* [nearly $90 million at 2010 prices] *restricts the activities of precisely those entrepreneurs who are most successful in filling the wants of consumers.*[10]

---

[8] Thomas Piketty, Les Hauts Revenus en France au XX siecle (Paris : Grasset, 2001), 548.
[9] Ludwig von Mises, Human Action, 840.
[10] Ibid., 806.

A second link: Austrians argue that inequalities resulting from the operation of the free market cannot be called unjust; see Hayek's remarks on this theme in Chapter 7. It follows that, in a free-market economy, there is no reason to deplore inequalities, let alone try to mitigate them, on grounds of justice.

A third link: attempts to reduce inequalities usually take the form of *progressive taxation*, i.e., higher tax rates on the richer citizens to finance benefits for the poorer. This policy is condemned by Austrians on the ground that it offends against the principle of citizens' equality before the law. It is argued that this principle means that everyone must pay the same rate of tax on his or her income.

In practice, however, even a modest income tax rate – say, 20% – would cause extreme hardship if imposed upon the entire income of a very poor taxpayer. Therefore, it is usual to set a 'threshold' below which no tax is payable; but this clearly offends against the aforesaid principle. If it is fair and reasonable to deviate from the principle at the bottom end of the scale, why not at the top?

Austrian economics has encouraged the belief, increasingly prevalent since the 1970s, that exorbitant inequalities should be tolerated because they are an intrinsic part of a market economy; because they are not unjust; and because attempts to reduce them via the tax system are fundamentally objectionable.

To put it bluntly, Austrianism is an ideology that permits the richest individuals to justify their gargantuan incomes and wealth, and their favorable tax status, in high-sounding intellectual terms.

NATURAL RESOURCES

Austrian economics seems inconsistent with our pressing need to consume resources less wastefully. We have already noted how Mises assumed that natural resources are more abundant than labor; and that therefore one can always boost economic growth, and thus consumption of resources, sufficiently to keep everyone employed. We have seen also how Menger commended fully competitive trading on the ground that it motivates all enterprises to produce and sell as much as possible.

One may add that the continuing pursuit of higher labor productivity means that there is a constant need to develop new products so that workers displaced by productivity-enhancing businesses can find other means of earning a living. Since whatever we consume is being supplied with ever-diminishing input of labor, it follows that *we need to consume more and more in order to keep ourselves in employment.*

We see here a perverse inversion of the traditional economic order. In the past, we had to work in order that we could consume; today we have to consume in order that we may work. This situation leads to more and more wasteful and superfluous consumption. Yet we should be trying to consume less. The pursuit of labor productivity, hitherto the key to a more prosperous economy, is now leading us to a more wasteful economy.

PUBLIC SERVICES AND WELFARE

Austrian ideology exhibits a strong distaste for the public sector. It dislikes taxation, basically because even where it is in principle under democratic control, it is in practice a form of discretionary constraint exercised over citizens by politicians.

Therefore it is, in Hayek's terms, an intrusion upon citizens' freedom. For anarcho-capitalists such as Rothbard, taxation is quite simply theft. In general, therefore, Austrians demand that taxes be reduced to minimum levels. This usually leads to deterioration in public services.

The Austrian answer to this problem is that the public services should be privatized. For Rothbard, even the police, the armed forces, and the courts of law could and should be privatized. Leaving aside such eccentricities, there are real objections to privatizing many of the other public services.

American libertarians argue that health services can be financed by commercial insurance, but American experience demonstrates the weaknesses of this theory. Welfare matters such as unemployment benefits are generally difficult, or even impossible, to insure effectively on a commercial basis.

But Austrians are inclined to the view that unemployment insurance should not exist anyway, since (according to Mises) it generates a strong disincentive to work.

Although this might be true for a minority of idle scroungers, it is evident that most of the unemployed do not wish to remain so; their predicament is forced upon them, often at least in part as a consequence of Austrian economic policies. For these policies demand intense competition, no state support for industry (or even for failing banks), and priority for the avoidance of inflation rather than for growth.

Another consequence of all-out competition is the prevailing rapacity of business today. Whereas in the past, businesses were often content to earn *adequate* profits, today they go for *maximum possible* profits. They are therefore less willing, or able, to treat their workers decently and to act in the public interest, rather than solely for their own narrow advantage.

This is easily explained. Today, shares in stock-exchange listed companies are held largely by fund managers who compete very actively with each other to achieve maximum returns. These powerful investors press the managements of the companies to maximize their profits. Companies that fail to do so fall out of favor in the market; their shares sink to low prices, which attract takeover bids.

The 'free market in corporate control', that delights libertarians, is less than delightful for those who have to work for, or live with, inordinately profit-obsessed businesses.

1 0

THE VIRTUOUS REPUBLIC

When several villages are united in a single community, perfect and large
enough to be nearly or quite self-sufficing, the state comes into
existence, originating in the bare needs of life, and continuing
in existence for the sake of a good life.
ARISTOTLE[1]

The clash between the *false idea of freedom*, denounced by Aristotle,[2] and the concept of the virtuous republic goes back to ancient times.

Like Aristotle's misguided democrats, modern libertarians think that freedom means as little government as possible. They even consider the state as something inherently pernicious. They despise government and idealize the untrammeled self, freely seeking its own fulfillment, with minimum restraint by state regulation or social convention, and with little or no concern for the common good.

---

[1] Aristotle, POLITICS, Book I, 3 (1252b).
[2] Ibid., Book V, 136 (1310a).

149

JEWISH AND CHRISTIAN TEACHING
ON GOVERNMENT

By contrast, the Judaeo-Christian tradition has always emphasized the need for sound government, including the regulation of economic activities. From the Old Testament through the Christian era to the latest Papal documents, we can trace this continuous theme.

The Jewish View of Government

The Mosaic law (Torah) sets up an extensive system of rules of conduct, of which a considerable number are detailed regulations concerning economic matters; thus, for example:

> *You must not exploit a poor and needy wage-earner, be he one of your brothers or a foreigner resident in your community; you must pay him his wages each day, not allowing the sun to set before you do.* (DEUTERONOMY 24: 14 – 15)

> *When you buy a Hebrew slave, his service will last six years. In the seventh year he shall leave a free man without paying compensation.* (EXODUS 21: 2)

> *For six years will you sow your land and gather its produce, but in the seventh year you will let it lie fallow and forgo all produce from it, so that those of your people who are poor can take food from it and the wild animals eat what they have left.* (EXODUS 23: 10 – 11)

> *Land will not be sold absolutely, for the land belongs to me, and you are only strangers and guests of mine.* (LEVITICUS 25: 23) (NIV: *you are but aliens and my tenants*).

The last words of King David are eloquent on the theme of wise and just government:

He whose rule is upright on earth, who rules in the fear of God, is like the morning light at sunrise on a cloudless morning making the grass of the earth sparkle after rain. (2 SAMUEL 23: 3)

Professor Daniel Elazar (1934-1999), a renowned writer on Jewish political science, describes the Jewish understanding of the relationship between divine and human authority:

The universe and its parts are under divine sovereignty and hence all human institutions possess only delegated authority and powers ... the good political order is a complex of interlocking authorities, the legitimacy of which derives from covenant-established partnership between God and humanity ... covenanting makes divine authority concrete and human authority possible in this world.[3]

Early Christian Views

In the New Testament, we find various observations on respect for political authorities; for example:

Everyone is to obey the governing authorities, because there is no authority except from God. (ROMANS 13: 1)

I urge then, first of all that petitions, prayers, intercessions ... should be offered for everyone, for kings and others in authority, so that we may be able to live peaceful and quiet lives. (I TIMOTHY 2: 1 - 2)

In the fourth century, St John Chrysostom writes that:

For that there should be rulers, and some rule and others be ruled, and that all things should not just be carried on in confu-

---

[3] Prof. Daniel J. Elazar, "Judaism and Politics", in ENCYCLOPEDIA OF JUDAISM (Leyden: Brill, 2006), 1083.

sion, the people swaying like waves in this direction and that; this, I say, is a work of God's wisdom. [4]

According to his contemporary St Augustine:

> *The well-ordered concord of domestic obedience and domestic rule has a relation to the well-ordered concord of civic obedience and civic rule … the father of a family ought to frame his domestic rule in accordance with the law of the city, so that the household may be in harmony with the civic order.* [5]

In a previous chapter Augustine describes the domestic order:

> *Those who rule serve those whom they seem to command; for they rule not from a love of power, but from a sense of the duty they owe to others – not because they are proud of authority, but because they love mercy.* [6]

The Middle Ages

St Thomas held that, even if there had been no original sin, human society would have required just governance:

> *A free person can be directed by another, when the ruler directs the ruled for his own good, or for the common good. And it would have been so even in the state of innocence, for two reasons.*

> *Firstly, because man is naturally a social being, so human beings in the state of innocence would have lived socially. But a social life among many people is not possible, unless someone presides for the good of all, since many direct themselves towards many ends, but one to one end. Hence the Philosopher*

---

[4] St John Chrysostom, HOMILIES ON THE EPISTLE TO THE ROMANS, trans. J.B. Morris (Oxford: Parker, 1861), 393 (Homily 23).
[5] St Augustine, DE CIVITATE DEI, Book XIX, Chap. 16.
[6] Ibid., Chap. 14.

says, at the beginning of the Politics, that wherever many are directed to one objective, one will always find a single leader in charge.

Secondly, if one man was preeminent in knowledge and in the ministration of justice, it would be wrong for his talents not to be used for the benefit of others, as says St Peter, 'Each of you has received a special grace, so... put it at the service of others.'[7]

On the question of markets, Thomas's attitude is well known: he believed in the concept of *justum pretium* (just price) and laid down, as we have noted, the principle that *to sell anything for more than it is worth, or buy for less than it is worth, is in itself unjust and unlawful.*[8] Thomas admits, in the same article, that just prices are not capable of precise determination:

The just price of things is not determined with exactitude, but consists rather of a kind of estimate, so that a slight addition or subtraction would not seem to offend against the equality of justice.[9]

It is hard to argue that, according to Thomas, the just price is simply the market price; for, as we all know, price variations in markets are often by no means slight; they can be large, rapid, erratic; experience shows that markets often go to extremes and lose touch with reality.

In practice, it was not uncommon in the Middle Ages for wage rates, and prices of everyday necessities, to be fixed by magistrates, while craftsmen's guilds regulated the prices of their mem-

---

[7] St Thomas Aquinas, SUMMA THEOLOGICA, Prima, Q. 96, Art. 4. The reference to the Philosopher is to Aristotle, POLITICS, Book I, 6 (1254a). The citation from St. Peter is from I PETER 4: 10.
[8] St Thomas Aquinas, SUMMA THEOLOGICA, Secunda Secundae, Q. 77, Art. 1.
[9] Ibid.

bers' handiwork. The prevailing ideal was that prices should be stabilized at levels that were fair to both buyers and sellers. Such a notion is obnoxious to modern libertarians, who desire a world wherein there is no stability, where there are no brakes on the movement of prices, or on the rapidity of economic change.

A FREE ECONOMY
IS INHERENTLY UNSTABLE

One may compare an economy with the *series-wound DC motor*, a type of electric motor traditionally used to drive streetcars and subway trains; a robust and reliable workhorse that has been in common use worldwide, in transport and industry, for well over a century. But this machine, when in the workshop for overhaul or test, must never be allowed to run free on full power.[10] For, unattached to a vehicle with its restraining inertia, it will accelerate without limit until its center flies apart. Nobody wants an accident like that with a traction motor weighing a ton or two!

Deregulation Promotes Instability

The modern highly competitive, deregulated economy has more than a passing resemblance to that motor. Its activities tend to accelerate till they are out of control, and thus self-destructive – as we have seen recently in the world of finance. Without restraint, they are inherently unstable.

People think that regulation is necessary to prevent deliberate malfeasance; so it is, but that is not its only, or even main, justifica-

---

[10] See Edward Hughes, ELECTRICAL TECHNOLOGY, 6th edition (London: Longmans, 1987), 402-403; or any basic textbook on electrical engineering.

tion. The fundamental problem is that a fully deregulated economy has a built-in tendency to run amok, even if nobody is willfully crooked. It is a situation where unbridled and often destructive competition rules, and where those who are uncompetitive do not survive.

The self-destruction of the unrestrained electric motor does not mean that the motor is defective. It simply means that it cannot function properly without restraining inertia. Likewise, the malfunctions of the deregulated economy do not prove that capitalism is fundamentally rotten. They prove that the capitalism needs restraints and is self-destructive without them.

The marriage of competition with information technology is inherently prolific of accelerating change. The technology stimulates competition by letting us speedily compare products and prices worldwide; and competition repays the compliment by stimulating faster development in the technology, which, as it develops, opens the way to quicker innovation in design and production.

Here we have a circular process that feeds upon itself to produce ever-accelerating change. But are we happy to live with the consequences? The French philosopher Roger-Pol Droit comments:

> *For us, the face of chaos is no longer a vision of total destruction. Its features have become those of the unforeseeable, of a state of perpetual uncertainty, of disorder that has become an institution. So what are we to do? How do we think philosophically about possible rules of action in an uncontrollable world?*

What place remains for man in a whirlwind that he suffers from but in which he cannot live?[11]

The Need for Inertia

In the economy, we need rules and constraints to provide a degree of inertia, to prevent excessive, uncontrollable acceleration.

Our forbears in the mid-twentieth century, who ran the economies of their day under a mass of controls and restrictions, were not as foolish as it is now fashionable to think. Their economies were more stable than ours. And, I venture to suggest, most people were happier with that way of life than we are today with our libertarian chaos.

As St Thomas insisted, man would have needed government *even in a state of innocence.* Human nature, like the electric motor – or like a train that cannot run without the constraint of its rails – is simply too dynamic to be able to survive in the absence of constraints. Human energy, like electricity, needs direction and control, lest it become destructive of itself and of everything around it. This is not a consequence of Adam's fall, but an inherent characteristic of human beings.

The Rise of Laissez-Faire

Outright rejection of Thomist economic thought, with its emphasis on stable values, made its appearance in the arena of secular intellectual debate during the eighteenth century. The arguments of the classical economists gained widespread public support, dis-

---

[11] Roger-Pol Droit's review of Pierre Caye's book MORALE ET CHAOS in LE MONDE (Paris), 5 December 2008.

crediting the traditional regulatory practices of governments and guilds.

English legislation (the *Combination Acts* of 1799 and 1800) and its French equivalent (the *Loi Le Chapelier* of 1791) attempted to outlaw all cooperation between businesses, and between workers, to stabilize prices and wages. Government regulation likewise fell out of favor.

The nineteenth century, particularly in its earlier decades, became the original heyday of *laissez-faire*, to which 'golden age', as they see it, libertarians of our times yearn to return.

But this age was very far from golden for most working people. As we see today in developing countries, people moved in great numbers from rural villages into the expanding industrial towns, where they found employment, but generally on miserable terms.

A broadly-based counter-reaction against *laissez-faire* policies therefore got under way. It took many forms, ranging from Marxism to Catholic social doctrine. Here we propose a very brief overview of the development of this Catholic doctrine.

PIONEERS OF CATHOLIC SOCIAL DOCTRINE

Wilhelm von Ketteler

In Germany, Wilhelm von Ketteler (1811-1877), Bishop of Mainz, was a pioneer of this movement. He strongly supported the development of workers' associations or unions, and of industrial cooperatives, as well as state regulation of working conditions. A few of his comments from 1869:

*The fundamental characteristic which gives the workers' move-
ment its importance and significance ... is the theme of corpora-
tive association, with a view to putting the strength of unity at
the service of workers' interests.*

*The first consequence of unconstrained freedom in all sectors of
the economy has been to cast the workers into an almost despe-
rate situation. This is something that no-one can deny, not even
those who regard this unlimited liberty as necessary and who
cherish the conviction that it is salutary in the long run. The
suppression of all the former workers' corporations has completely isolated the worker and left him to shift for himself ...
human association has been destroyed and we have seen in its
place the formidable extension of financial association.* [12]

A message that has lost none of its relevance!

The bishop proposed several major objectives for workers' associations: *an increase in wages to correspond with the true value of
work* [emphasis added; note the total negation of Austrian atti-
tudes]; reduction in working hours; obligatory days of rest; prohi-
bition of the employment of children, and of mothers of young
families.

Henri-Dominique Lacordaire OP

In France, the theme of opposition to *laissez-faire* was taken up
by Fr. Lacordaire (1802-1861), a Dominican who re-established his
order in France and became a member of the *Académie Française*.
An eloquent orator, he gave a famous series of lectures at Notre-
Dame de Paris, in one of which he takes up, in 1848, a theme that is

---

[12] Bishop Wilhelm von Ketteler, sermon given on 25 July 1869 at Offenbach am Main;
see "*Die Arbeiterbewegung und ihr Streben*" in Ketteler, SCHRIFTEN, AUFSÄTZE UND
REDEN 1867 – 1870 (Mainz: von Hase und Koehler, 1978), 406 – 428.

topical again in France today: Sunday working. According to a French law of 1814, cessation of work on Sundays was supposed to be obligatory, but in the mid-nineteenth century this rule was largely disregarded.

> *Do you wish to rupture the equilibrium of human activity, to bring about the degradation of souls, the oppression of the weak, the greed of all and the misery of the majority? Is that what you want? You have only to disregard the law of work as it was enacted in the act of creation; increase temporal work, forcibly diminish spiritual work; abandon man to his greed and to the will of his masters; do that, and you can be sure of reaping in a generation the fruit that will satisfy you, if you love the moral and physical degradation of humanity.*[13]

Lacordaire reminds his audience that the fourth commandment states explicitly that one of the reasons for the rule against work on the Sabbath is to allow employees to take a break from their labors: *so that your servants … may rest as you do.*[14]

He castigates those who argued that, according to then current French law, no-one was obliged to work on Sundays. In practice, he says, people have little choice, so such arguments are hypocritical.

> *Ask the laborer if he is free to stop work at dawn on the day when he is supposed to rest … Ask those withered beings who people the industrial quarters, if they are free to save their souls while resting their bodies.*[15]

---

[13] Henri-Dominique Lacordaire OP, DU DOUBLE TRAVAIL DE L'HOMME (52nd Conférence de Notre-Dame, Paris, 1848), 238.

[14] Ibid., 239. He refers to DEUTERONOMY 5: 14.

[15] Ibid., 245.

And he winds up his peroration with a memorable sentence, which sums up much of what is wrong with the doctrine of untrammeled market freedom:

> *Between the strong and the weak, between rich and poor, between master and servant, it is liberty that is oppressive and the law that sets free.*[16]

Cardinal Henry Manning

In England, Cardinal Manning (1808-1892), Archbishop of Westminster, a convert from the Church of England, was an enthusiastic campaigner for workers' rights; he was involved in the drafting of Leo XIII's encyclical RERUM NOVARUM (1891). Manning argued in favor of worker solidarity, legislative regulation of workplaces, tribunals to arbitrate in industrial disputes.

> *It is clear that there can be no real free contract between the capitalist and the worker. The capitalist wears golden armor; and the worker, if he remains obstinate, knows that hunger awaits him. Thus the 'free contract' has become the employers' gospel; that is why they are so indignant at the idea of intervention by an arbitrator; and why they have protested against all outside interference in their private affairs.*[17]

Msgr. John A. Ryan

In America, Msgr. Ryan (1869-1945) published the first volume of A LIVING WAGE in 1906. Here he criticized severely the tendency of the Enlightenment economists and their followers – he calls

---

[16] Ibid., 246.

[17] Cardinal Henry Manning, THE LABOUR AND SOCIAL QUESTION, Chap. IV (London, 1891); Manning, LA QUESTION OUVRIERE ET SOCIALE (Paris: Tolra, 1892), 98.

them the *Revolutionists* – to try to reform society by going back to an imaginary 'state of nature' in which there had been (as they supposed) little or nothing in the way of constraints and regulations.

> As the late Professor Ritchie has well said: 'To the Thomist, the law of nature is an ideal for human law; to the Rousseauist it is an ideal to be reached by getting rid of human law altogether.' In the mind of the Revolutionist, therefore, to re-establish the law of nature meant to shake off the cumbersome and obstructive political regulations of the day, and get back to the simple state of nature, the semi-anarchical conditions of primitive times.
>
> This was, of course, a very inadequate interpretation of man's nature and of the natural law ... Nevertheless, upon it were based and by it was measured men's natural rights in the Revolutionary system. As a consequence, the rights of the individual were exaggerated and the rights of society minimized. In practice this juristic liberalism has meant, and always will mean, that the State allows to the strong the legal right and power to oppress the weak. A good example of the evil is to be found in the results of the economic policy of laissez-faire.[18]

Observe how Ryan's thought (1906) on the economic role of the law echoes that of Lacordaire (1848). The demolition of the edifice of libertarianism, as it stood in the middle of the nineteenth century, was by no means complete sixty years later. And now, we are once again confronted by the need to knock down this 'heresy'.

---

[18] Msgr John A. Ryan, A LIVING WAGE (New York : Macmillan, 1906), 63. The citation at the beginning is from David George Ritchie (1853-1902), professor at Oxford and later at St Andrews, in NATURAL RIGHTS (London : Sonnenschein, 1895), 43.

Let us hope that, this time, the task does not take well over half a century.

Papal Teachings: Leo XIII

From RERUM NOVARUM (1891) onwards, a whole series of Vatican documents pursues our theme. Leo XIII, while condemning secular socialism, has much to say on the role and duties of the state in the creation of a just society; for example:

> *The foremost duty, therefore, of the rulers of the State should be to make sure that the laws and institutions shall ... realize public well-being and private prosperity ... it lies in the power of a ruler to benefit every class in the State, and amongst the rest to promote to the utmost the interests of the poor ... It would be irrational to neglect one portion of the citizens and favor another, and therefore the public administration must duly and solicitously provide for the welfare and comfort of the working classes; otherwise, that law of justice will be violated which ordains that each man should have his due ... Justice, therefore, demands that the interests of the working classes should be carefully watched over by the administration, so that they who contribute so largely to the advantage of the community may themselves share in the benefits which they create.*[19]

Leo goes on to point out that the determination of wages purely by agreement between employer and employee in a free market may not be adequate.

> *Wages, as we are told, are regulated by free consent, and therefore the employer, when he pays what was agreed upon, has*

---

[19] Pope Leo XIII, encyclical RERUM NOVARUM (1891), Pars. 32-34.

done his part and seemingly is not called upon to do anything beyond.[20]

However,

Man's labor is necessary; for without the result of labor a man cannot live, and self-preservation is a law of nature, which it is wrong to disobey ... It necessarily follows that each one has a natural right to procure what is required in order to live, and the poor can procure that in no other way than by what they can earn through their work.[21]

Therefore,

Let the working man and the employer make free agreements, and in particular let them agree freely as to the wages; nevertheless, there underlies a dictate of natural justice more imperious and ancient than any bargain between man and man, namely, that wages ought not to be insufficient to support a frugal and well-behaved wage-earner. If through necessity or fear of a worse evil the workman accept harder conditions because an employer or contractor will afford him no better, he is made the victim of force and injustice.[22]

Leo recommends that if just wages cannot be obtained by 'free agreements', then the best remedy will generally be for workers to combine in associations or unions to strengthen their position, *the State being appealed to, should circumstances require, for its sanction and protection.* He continues: *the most important (associations) of all are workingmen's unions, for these virtually include all the rest.*[23] Moreover,

---

[20] Ibid., Par. 43.
[21] Ibid., Par. 44.
[22] Ibid., Par. 45.
[23] Ibid., Par. 49.

163

To enter into a "society" of this kind is the natural right of man; and the State has for its office to protect natural rights, not to destroy them; and, if it forbid its citizens to form associations, it contradicts the very principle of its own existence, for both they and it exist in virtue of the like principle, namely, the natural tendency of man to dwell in society.[24]

Pius XI

In QUADRAGESIMO ANNO (1931), Pius XI seems at least as hostile to 'liberals' (libertarians and free-marketeers) as to socialists. He begins with a retrospective glance at the troubles that had inspired Leo to write RERUM NOVARUM. Pius is quite sarcastic at the expense of believers in the 'law of the market':

One class, very small in numbers, was enjoying almost all the advantages which modern inventions so abundantly provided; the other, embracing the huge multitude of working people, oppressed by wretched poverty, was vainly seeking escape from the straits wherein it stood.

Quite agreeable, of course, was this state of things to those who thought their abundant riches the result of inevitable economic laws and accordingly, as if it were for charity to veil the violation of justice which lawmakers not only tolerated but at times sanctioned, wanted the whole care of supporting the poor committed to charity alone.[25]

The very Austrian School attitude here condemned by Pius matches with startling precision the content of countless libertarian websites today. Pius continues with a forceful denunciation of libertarian anti-statism:

---

[24] Ibid., Par. 52.
[25] Pope Pius XI, encyclical QUADRAGESIMO ANNO (1931), Pars. 3 & 4.

*Leo XIII, breaking through the confines imposed by Liberalism
[libertarianism], fearlessly taught that government must not
be thought a mere guardian of law and of good order ... A new
branch of law, wholly unknown to the earlier time, has arisen
from this continuous and unwearied labor to protect vigorously
the sacred rights of the workers that flow from their dignity as
men and as Christians.*[26]

This, of course, is precisely what Hayek thought should not happen. He objected in principle to new positive legislation.

Pius emphasized the sanctity in principle of private property, but insists that it must not be exploited in ways that are damaging to the public good.

*Yet when the State brings private ownership into harmony with
the needs of the common good, it does not commit a hostile act
against private owners but rather does them a friendly service;
for it thereby effectively prevents the private possession of goods
... from causing intolerable evils and thus rushing to its own
destruction.*[27]

Pius flatly rejects the theory, normal among Austrian and neoclassical economists, that labor is simply a commodity like any other whose value is to be determined purely by the interplay of supply and demand in unconstrained markets.

*Labor ... is not a mere commodity. On the contrary, the worker's human dignity in it must be recognized. It cannot therefore
be bought and sold like a commodity. In the first place, the
worker must be paid a wage sufficient to support him and his
family. The right ordering of economic life cannot be left to a
free competition of forces. For from this source, as from a poi-*

---

[26] Ibid., Pars. 25 & 28.
[27] Ibid., Par. 49.

soned spring, have originated and spread all the errors of the individualist economic teaching.[28]

Striking at the heart of Austrian doctrine, Pius explicitly repudiates one of its most fundamental ideas: the theory of *spontaneous order*, as Hayek called it. This theory, as Pius explains, holds that

> ... *economic life must be considered and treated as altogether free from and independent of public authority, because in the market, i.e. in the free struggle of competitors, it would have a principle of self-direction which governs it much more perfectly than would the intervention of any created intellect.*[29]

The theory, Pius tells us, has been condemned by its bad consequences. That was surely clear enough in 1931, but too many economists still have not learned the lesson. They persist in trying to thrust upon us this doctrine that was discredited before most of us were born.

Vatican Council II

In GAUDIUM ET SPES (1965) we read that

> *The political community and public authority are founded on human nature and hence belong to the order designed by God ... political authority must always be exercised within the limits of the moral order and directed towards the common good ... the complex circumstances of our day make it necessary for public authority to intervene more often in social, economic and cultural matters.*[30]

---

[28] Ibid., Pars. 83, 71 and 88 respectively for the three quotations. Note again in the third quote the source for the title of this book.

[29] Ibid., Par. 88.

[30] Vatican Council II, GAUDIUM ET SPES (1965) [Pastoral Constitution of the Church in the Contemporary World], Pars. 74 – 75.

Pope John Paul II

In LABOREM EXERCENS, Pope John Paul II observes that

For certain supporters of materialistic and economistic thought, work was understood and treated as a sort of 'merchandise' that the worker... sells to the employer, who at the same time is the possessor of the capital, that is to say, of all the working tools and means that make production possible. This way of looking at work was widespread especially in the first half of the nineteenth century. Since then, explicit expressions of this sort have almost disappeared, and have given way to more human ways of thinking about work and evaluating it.[31]

Sadly, this progress that the Pope noted with approval has been largely undone in recent years by the materialist economists, particularly the Austrians. They have deliberately sought to reinstate early nineteenth-century ideas and even to render them more harmful, notably through their heavy emphasis on the subjectivity of value.

The Pope complains that there has been a reversal of the order ordained by God: in economic theory, *man is treated as an instrument of production.* He continues:

We must first of all recall a principle that has always been taught by the Church: the principle of the priority of labor over capital ... labor is always a primary efficient cause, while capital, the whole collection of means of production, remains a mere instrument or instrumental cause.[32]

John Paul reemphasizes the importance of labor unions, while insisting that they should pursue the positive goal of fair treatment

---

[31] Pope John Paul II, encyclical LABOREM EXERCENS (1981), Par. 7.
[32] Ibid., Par. 8.

for their members, rather than the negative goal of attacking capitalists as a class:

> *Unions… are indeed a mouthpiece for the struggle for social justice, for the just rights of working people in accordance with their individual professions. However, this struggle should be seen as a normal endeavor 'for' the just good: in the present case, for the good which corresponds to the needs and merits of working people associated by profession; but it is not a struggle 'against' others.*[33]

In CENTESIMUS ANNUS (1991), John Paul observes that many people still live

> *… in situations in which the rules of the earliest period of capitalism still flourish in conditions of 'ruthlessness' in no way inferior [nullo atrocitate minor, which translates literally as 'no less in atrocity'] to the darkest moments of the first phase of industrialization.*[34]

Although this stark description applies mainly to 'Third World' countries, the Pope notes that *aspects typical of the Third World also appear in developed countries*, and he notes that these conditions are frequently caused by *the constant transformation of the methods of production and consumption*, as a result of which *those who fail to keep up with the times can easily be marginalized*.[35]

This comment points to an inherent problem of unfettered capitalism: the ferocity of competition leads to an excessively rapid pace of change, and the difficulty of adapting thereto leads to many people 'failing to keep up with the times'. The 'dynamic'

---

[33] Ibid., Par. 20.
[34] CENTESIMUS ANNUS , Par. 33.
[35] Ibid.

(euphemism for unstable) economy that free-marketeers love creates too many casualties.

Turning to possible alternatives to the present malfunctioning capitalist system, the Pope calls for a society that

> ... is not directed against the market, but demands that the market be appropriately controlled by the forces of society and by the State, so as to guarantee that the basic needs of the whole of society are satisfied.[36]

Finally, we note John Paul's warning:

> Certainly, the mechanisms of the market offer secure advantages ... nevertheless, these mechanisms carry the risk of an 'idolatry' of the market, an idolatry which ignores the existence of goods which by their nature are not and cannot be mere commodities.[37]

In practice this 'idolatry' manifests itself in the view, normal among free-marketeers, that the market is always right, the market's valuation of anything is always the true value, so one cannot argue with it.

Pope Benedict XVI

In DEUS CARITAS EST (2005), Benedict does not discuss markets, but has much to say about the state.

The Pope vigorously insists on the essential role of the state in the construction of a just society.

> The pursuit of justice must be a fundamental norm of the state ... the aim of a just social order is to guarantee to each person

---

[36] Ibid., Par. 35.

[37] Ibid., Par. 40. This paragraph in the official English translation appears to contain a mistranslation, where it states that the mechanisms of the market 'offer secure advantages.' The Latin text has *multa praebent auxilia*, which literally translated means 'offer many advantages (or aids).'

… his share of the community's goods … The formation of just
structures is not directly the duty of the Church, but belongs to
the world of politics, the sphere of the autonomous use of rea-
son.[38]

In CARITAS IN VERITATE (2009), Benedict takes up the implica-
tions for the market economy:

The social doctrine of the Church has unceasingly highlighted
the importance of distributive justice *and* social justice *for the*
market economy, not only because it belongs within a broader
social and political context, but also because of the wider net-
work of relations within which it operates. In fact, if the market
is governed solely by the principle of the equivalence in value of
exchanged goods, it cannot produce the social cohesion that it
requires in order to function well … It is … erroneous to hold
that the market economy has an inbuilt need for a quota of pov-
erty and underdevelopment in order to function at its best. It is
in the interests of the market to promote emancipation, but in
order to do so effectively, it cannot rely only on itself, because it
is not able to produce by itself something that lies outside its
competence.[39]

This discourse is far removed indeed from the vision of most
economists of the Austrian School, with their contempt for the
state and the political process; their naïve belief that the sum of
every individual's self-seeking actions will add up to a good society for everyone; their strange conceit that an unregulated market
dominated by greedy, myopic speculators could offer a better
means of guidance for society than a well-run and beneficent public administration.

---

[38] Pope Benedict XVI, encyclical DEUS CARITAS EST (2005), Pars. 26, 29.
[39] Pope Benedict XVI, encyclical CARITAS IN VERITATE (2009), Par. 35.

AUSTRIAN SCHOOL OFFERS
COUNSEL OF DESPAIR

To understand Austrianism we must see it in its historical context; it began in a world dominated by the fear that Communism or, later, Nazism or fascism, might take over Europe and impose their own evidently unacceptable kinds of order. The Austrians proposed to avoid that disaster by, so far as possible, dismantling the state. Since they had to put some form of guidance system in its place, they opted for the impersonal force of the unconstrained market, which would not, by definition, interfere with freedom as they perversely defined it.

But this is counsel of despair. It writes off as hopeless the quest for good government, to which, however, Catholic doctrine insists that there is no viable alternative. In reality, the only way to achieve such freedom and justice as is attainable in this imperfect world, is to press on with the difficult, never-ending task of striving to build and maintain the virtuous republic.

LIBERTARIAN CATHOLICISM?

*Democratic capitalism calls forth not only a new
theology, but a new type of religion.*
MICHAEL NOVAK[1]

Though the gulf between the Austrian economists and mainstream Catholicism yawns wide, certain neoconservative
Catholics have striven to bridge it, and thus to demonstrate that
Catholic doctrine can, and should, be so interpreted as to legitim-
ize libertarian capitalism. We examine below the ideas of some
leading exponents of this 'libertarian Catholicism.'

MICHAEL NOVAK

Michael Novak (born 1933) holds a Chair of Religion, Philosophy and Politics at the American Enterprise Institute. He has published many books, the earliest of which show a left-of-centre
orientation which, it would seem, he has long since abandoned.

---

[1] Novak, THE SPIRIT OF DEMOCRATIC CAPITALISM (New York: American Enterprise
Institute/Simon & Schuster, 1982), 69.

Today, he defends many libertarian economic tenets and insists that these can be compatible with Catholic teaching. Or, to be more precise, he insists that Catholic teaching ought to be compatible with his views, but in certain matters is not, due to regrettable European influences.

Thus, in an article published on a website linked with The Faith and Reason Institute, Novak observes that:

> *During my lifetime, Catholic Social Doctrine has been far too much distorted by being formulated through the lens of European experience, especially feudal, class-bound experience on the one hand, and social democratic experience on the other. That lens is a bit more pink than natural color. We in America are indebted to Europe; but we also have the experience of a New World. It is our task to contribute new things to the universal patrimony of the Catholic people.* [2]

Novak avoids the purely negative Austrian definition of freedom. For him,

> *True liberty is ordered liberty; temperance, fortitude, a sense of proportion* (justice) *and practical wisdom are ... cardinal habits* [that] *give order to our capacity for human freedom.* [3]

Here we have a positive concept not so far removed from that of the Catechism. However, the individualist Novak argues that justice comes only from individual self-discipline and cannot be imposed from above.

---

[2] Novak, "The Adventure of Catholic Social Doctrine" (5 June 2008) available online at: *http://www.thecatholicthing.org/2008/the-adventure-of-catholic-social-doctrine.html* (accessed 1 July 2010).

[3] Novak, THIS HEMISPHERE OF LIBERTY (Washington, DC: American Enterprise Institute Press, 1990), 117.

But compare DIGNITATIS HUMANAE: *the protection and promotion of the inviolable rights of man ranks among the essential duties of government.*[4]

For Novak, 'social justice' means citizens working together voluntarily to *put up a school together,* to *hold a bake sale for some charitable cause,* to *clean up the environment* and so on.[5] Hayek favored such voluntary action, but did not call it "social justice"; he reserved that term for attempts (which he abhorred) by the state to construct a just social order.[6]

Novak holds that *social justice is a virtue that can be exercised solely by individuals.*[7] This makes better sense than Hayek's fantasy, the society that does not need good people to run it.

But Novak insists that we must work towards a better society through voluntary action, not through political and legislative process. The latter should merely provide a framework within which virtuous individuals can spontaneously create a just society, *only as a last resort, when all else fails, through turning to the state.*[8]

But there are serious practical obstacles to achieving a just society purely through individual good behavior. For instance, if unscrupulous entrepreneurs pay grossly inadequate wages, benevolent employers may be unable to do much better, since their higher costs would make them uncompetitive with the rascals. Regulation of wages may therefore be necessary.

---

[4] Vatican Council II, DIGNITATIS HUMANAE (1965), Declaration on Religious Freedom, Par. 6.

[5] Novak, THREE IN ONE: ESSAYS ON DEMOCRATIC CAPITALISM (Lanham, Maryland: Madison Books, 2000), 131.

[6] Hayek, THE MIRAGE OF SOCIAL JUSTICE, passim.

[7] Novak, THREE IN ONE, 133.

[8] Novak, ON CULTIVATING LIBERTY (Lanham, Maryland: Rowman & Littlefield, 1999), 76.

Benedict XVI in DEUS CARITAS EST eschews anti-statism, distinguishing clearly between the roles of the state and of voluntary Christian charity:

> *The Church cannot and must not take upon herself the political battle to bring about the most just society possible. She cannot and must not replace the State.*[9]

The problems of the hypercompetitive society find little recognition in Novak, whose account of competition – *the natural play of the free person* – is wholeheartedly favorable.[10] Against those who object to Mises' 'every penny a ballot-paper' theory, Novak argues that *corporations which seek mass markets have a far larger economic base* than those which cater to the rich.[11]

Official statistics disagree. They show that half of all US personal income goes to 20% of households,[12] while half of all personal wealth is held by well below 10% of households.[13] Mises' 'market democracy' is, in reality, a plutocracy in which minorities hold the majority of 'votes'. A society in which 'voting' is based on spending power, rather than on the democratic principle of one person one vote, will inevitably be a society that caters more to the caprices of the rich than to the needs of the poor.

---

[9] Pope Benedict XVI, encyclical DEUS CARITAS EST (2006), Par. 28.

[10] Novak, THE SPIRIT OF DEMOCRATIC CAPITALISM, Chap. 20, 347.

[11] Ibid., Chap. 5, part 2.

[12] US Census Bureau (HHES) HISTORICAL INCOME TABLES (2001), Table IE-3.

[13] Arthur B. Kennickell (Federal Reserve Board), A ROLLING TIDE: CHANGES IN THE DISTRIBUTION OF WEALTH IN THE US, 1989 – 2001. This paper suggests that US personal wealth in 2001 could be attributed "about a third each to the wealthiest 1%, the next 9% and the remaining 90% of the population". Thus it appears that the top 10% hold two-thirds of total wealth; accordingly the majority (just over 50%) thereof is held by well below 10% of the total population. The paper is available online at: *www.federalreserve.gov/pubs/oss/oss2/papers/concentration.2001.10.pdf* (accessed 1 July 2010).

The United States has been built up by generations of immigrants who saw America as a refuge from oppressive societies dominated by privileged minorities. Now Americans have created for themselves a society dominated by a small minority of hyper-opulent entrepreneurs and investors. And they have done this with the encouragement of scions of the imperial Austrian aristocracy!

Novak, following Hayek and Mises, gives low priority to distributive justice. *Under democratic capitalism, inequalities of wealth and power are not considered evil in themselves ... nature itself generates inequalities.*[14] And again, *It is not unjust if some acorns fail to become oaks.*[15] Compare the Vatican's COMPENDIUM OF SOCIAL DOCTRINE:

> *Each person must have access to the level of well-being that is necessary for his full development ... property rights and the right of free trade must be subordinated to this norm (the universal destination of goods).*[16]

Elsewhere, Benedict XVI affirms that *it is right to foster equality in the distribution of wealth in the world.*[17] Novak argues that *the ethics of justice have shifted decisively from distributive justice to productive justice ... the latter is the precondition of the former.* He propounds *the moral imperative of sufficient productivity.*[18]

This means that the top priority is to increase output, so that there will be more for everybody; an argument reminiscent of

---

[14] Novak, THE SPIRIT OF DEMOCRATIC CAPITALISM, 84.

[15] Novak, THREE IN ONE, 126.

[16] Pontifical Council for Justice and Peace, COMPENDIUM OF THE SOCIAL DOCTRINE OF THE CHURCH (Città del Vaticano : Libreria Editrice Vaticana, 2004), Par. 172.

[17] Pope Benedict XVI, Address to H.E. Valentin Bizhilev (Bulgarian Ambassador to the Holy See), May 13 2006.

[18] Novak, THREE IN ONE, 48.

Menger's comments on competition (see Chapter 5) and dear to defenders of libertarian capitalism. It accords ill with the evidence of recent American history: despite robust growth, inequalities have widened, poverty and insecurity have become more widespread.

Nor does it meet today's urgent need to curb the environmental ravages of economic expansion. Novak denies that there are real limits to growth;[19] he decries those who see social justice as a "zero-sum game" of distributing fairly a limited pool of riches.[20] But ecologists warn that the human race is already consuming the earth's resources at a more than sustainable pace, even though many people are still extremely poor.[21] So it would seem that there are indeed certain limits to economic growth, implying a need to spread available resources more evenly.

ROBERT A. SIRICO

Fr. Robert Sirico (born 1951) is founder and president of the Acton Institute, a libertarian think-tank named after the English Catholic politician and historian John Emerich Acton (1834-1902), first Baron Acton of Aldenham. Sirico is a vehement campaigner for *laissez-faire* economic and social policies and for the Austrian School. Prominent in his thinking is a certain contempt, which

---

[19] Ibid., Chap. 6, passim.
[20] Novak, SPIRIT OF DEMOCRATIC CAPITALISM, Chap. 5, passim.
[21] The World Wildlife Fund's LIVING PLANET Report gives a detailed analysis covering practically every country in the world. This shows that the "ecological footprint" of the entire human race (in 2005) was "1.3 planets", i.e., that overall consumption of natural resources is running at a rate 30% more than sustainable. Available at: *http://assets.panda.org/downloads/living_planet_report.pdf* (accessed 1 July 2010).

would seem to be unbiblical and un-Catholic, for the role of law in society:

> *If we are required to do anything by law, and thereby forced by public authority to undertake some action, we comply because we must ... the impulse here is essentially one of fear.* [22]

Sirico apparently sees no merit in complying with the law, since (he asserts) we do so only from fear of punishment. By contrast, according to the distinguished Catholic theologian Joseph Pohle,

> *Not only are more perfect works of supererogation ... good and meritorious, but also works of obligation, such as faithful observance of the commandments, as Jesus says (Matt. 19:17): if thou wilt enter into life, keep the commandments.* [23]

Sirico appears to hold a curious misconception of the noble theme of law and justice. The law, as the CATECHISM observes, *is a rule of conduct enacted by competent authorities for the sake of the common good,* [24] following St Thomas: *law is properly, firstly and principally directed towards the common good.* [25] We may contrast Sirico's attitude with that of the psalmist: *And I will walk at liberty, for I seek thy precepts...and I will delight myself in thy commandments, which I have loved.* [26] Except where a law is blatantly unjust, and therefore in principle invalid, [27] living according to the law normally contributes, as St Thomas says, to the common good.

---

[22] Robert Sirico, "Mandated Giving Doesn't Come from the Heart," RELIGION AND LIBERTY, Vol. 17, no. 4 (Fall 2007) (Grand Rapids, Michigan: Acton Institute), 14.
[23] Prof. Joseph Pohle, "Merit", THE CATHOLIC ENCYCLOPEDIA (New York : Appleton, 1907-1912),
[24] CATECHISM OF THE CATHOLIC CHURCH, Par. 1951.
[25] St Thomas Aquinas, SUMMA THEOLOGICA, Prima Secundae, Q. 90, Art. 3.
[26] Psalm 119 : 45, 47 (KJV).
[27] St Augustine, DE LIBERO ARBITRIO, I, 5: *that which is not just seems to be no law at all.*

That is why the psalmist evokes a willing and heartfelt respect for the law, the sentiment that abiding by the law actually helps one to be essentially free. How much 'freedom', in any normal understanding of the word, do we find in states where the rule of law is lacking? All this accords with the Catholic doctrine that *there is no true freedom except in the pursuit of what is good and just.*[28]

Sirico's negative view of compliance with the law, quoted above, arises in the context of redistributive taxation, that *bête noire* of the libertarians. Their economic strategies lead, as recent experience shows, to the growth of huge inequalities; yet they insist that no attempt be made to use the tax system to correct these imbalances.

A favorite argument for this view is that, if inequalities are reduced via the tax system, then the rich are being forced to give to the poor; so there is, from the givers' point of view, no merit in doing so; as Sirico writes,

> *A government program effects nothing toward fulfilling the Gospel requirement that we give of our own time and income towards assisting the poor.*[29]

Libertarians often get angry about such programs. It is hard to avoid the suspicion that many of them are successful, affluent people who have made or acquired fortunes, but object to being asked to pay away more than a trifle in taxes.

Their argument is perverse, for two reasons. Firstly, it implies that a prime reason for transferring money from rich to poor is that the rich gain merit by transferring it voluntarily. But, to be practic-

---

[28] CATECHISM OF THE CATHOLIC CHURCH, Par. 1733.
[29] Sirico, "Mandated Giving."

al, the basic purpose of such transfers is to help the poor, not to allow the rich to gain special merit by acts of supererogation. That is why, in the Jewish tradition from biblical times to our own, assistance to the poor has always been considered to be basically a legal obligation, not a voluntary offering. In other words, essentially a tax. Secondly, it is wrong to assume that there is no merit in paying willingly and cheerfully our tax contributions toward the relief of poverty.

It is interesting to look briefly at traditional Jewish doctrine and practice in this matter:

> *The following system of relief was established in Mishnaic times* [approximately the first and second centuries AD]. *Every community had a charity-box (kuppah) containing the funds for the support of the indigent townsmen … the charity-box was given in charge of three trustees … for the collection of the money two men of the utmost respectability were sent, endowed with full power to tax the people and to seize property until the full sum required was given them.*[30]

Moreover, according to the Talmud, residence in a city for three months obliged persons to contribute to the *kuppah*.[31]

> *The view that redistribution to mitigate excessive inequalities is a legal obligation, not simply something that one is encouraged to do out of the kindness of one's heart, thus has its origins in Jewish tradition; and it carries forward into Catholic teaching:*

---

[30] Rabbi Dr. Kaufmann Kohler, THE JEWISH ENCYCLOPEDIA (New York: KTAV, 1901 – 1906), article "Charity". The word 'charity' in this context translates the Hebrew *tzedakah*, whose basic meaning is 'justice'.

[31] BABA BATHRA (Babylonian Talmud), Chap. I, Folio 8a; see *www.comeandhear.com* (Accessed 1 July 2010).

the giving of what is due in justice is not to be represented as the offering of a charitable gift.[32]

That little sentence flattens in a few succinct words the libertarian argument. None of this implies that obligatory assistance to the poor or otherwise disadvantaged could or should supersede the need for charitable giving.

Caritas will always prove necessary, even in the most just society, as we are reminded by Benedict XVI.[33] But the task of achieving a tolerably fair basic pattern of incomes is not, in either Jewish or Catholic doctrine, a matter to be left to voluntary handouts by individuals. As the Pope tells us in the same encyclical,

> *The direct duty to work for a just ordering of society ... is proper to the lay faithful. As citizens of the State, they are called to take part in public life in a personal capacity. So they cannot relinquish their participation "in the many different economic, social, legislative, administrative and cultural areas, which are intended to promote organically and institutionally the common good."* [34]

No anti-statism here.

The creation of a just order in society *must be the achievement of politics* says the Pope.[35] It is a basic necessity, like ensuring that everyone drives in accordance with the rules of the road. We would not think of leaving that to the voluntary goodwill of motorists and truck-drivers. We insist that they stick to the rules, and we punish them if they do not. Even libertarians do not generally complain. But then, it does not cost them much to comply.

---

[32] Pope Paul VI, decree APOSTOLICAM ACTUOSITATEM (1965), Ch. II, Art. 8, Par. 5.

[33] Pope Benedict XVI, encyclical DEUS CARITAS EST (2006), Par. 28.

[34] Ibid., Par. 29

[35] Ibid., Par. 28.

In another article, ambiguously titled "Minimum Wage, Maximum Suffering," Sirico trots out familiar neoconservative arguments against minimum wage legislation.[36] His argument: it is not the payment of tiny wages, but the law against this abuse, that causes maximum suffering. How so? Because, in his view, any regulatory downside limit on wage rates reduces the number of jobs on offer and so leads to higher unemployment; for each employer has a fixed amount available to spend on remuneration.

On this view, one would have to favor upside limits to curb excessive top-level pay, since such limits would free up cash for more, or better-paid, employment at the lower levels! But one seldom hears this argument from libertarians. They are normally on the side of the fattest cats.

In fact, the case against deregulated labor markets, in certain situations, has been made even by Mises himself; he argues (see Chapter 6) that, in an economy where labor is abundant (relative to other factors of production), a truly free labor market will lead to starvation wages. However, the problem is wider than that. Even if there is no general oversupply of labor, a contract between an individual employee and an employer is usually a contract between parties of unequal strength.

As a general rule, even if an employer is an individual householder or sole trader, he or she is richer than the employees, often older, more knowledgeable and experienced, and does not need to close a deal instantly in order to survive. In the common situation where the employer is a large corporation, the difference in bar-

---

[36] Sirico, "Minimum Wage, Maximum Suffering", Acton Institute website (15 August 2007). Available at: *www.acton.org/commentary/commentary397.php* (accessed 1 July 2010).

gaining power between the employer and a single employee is obvious. 'Freely negotiated' contracts between parties of unequal strength tend to be unjust, hence the need for regulation. In this matter, the libertarians are fighting against common sense.

THOMAS E. WOODS, JR.

Thomas Woods (born 1972), formerly a professor of history at the State University of New York, is today a senior fellow of the Ludwig von Mises Institute.

He is a prolific writer on economic and religious themes. His book THE CHURCH AND THE MARKET is a widely-read recent contribution to the literature of neoconservative Catholicism.[37]

Like Novak and Sirico, Woods is strongly anti-statist. In an earlier work, THE CHURCH CONFRONTS MODERNITY, he finds fault with the Thomist view of the state, though in general he claims to follow St Thomas.

It is of considerable significance that St Thomas and the Scholastics should have rejected the theory of the state held by, for example, St Augustine[38] – namely, that the state came into existence as a result of original sin. Aquinas denied that the state was merely a necessary evil, arguing instead that even if man had not fallen ... government would still be both necessary and just. It is significant that this came to be the dominant view within the Church, since a philosophy that placed the origins of the state in the consequences of iniquity was much less likely to

---

[37] Woods, THE CHURCH AND THE MARKET (Lanham, Maryland: Lexington, 2005).
[38] St Augustine wrote (De CIVITATE DEI, Book XIX, Chap. 15) that *God wished his rational creatures, made in his own image, to rule only over the irrational creation – not man over man, but man over beast.* However, Augustine clearly acknowledges, in his preceding chapter, the need for and possibility of good government in a fallen world. (See Chapter 10 supra.)

emphasize the state's positive role in securing the common good.[39]

Woods is an admirer of the anarchist Rothbard, and of the Austrian economists in general. In his preface to THE CHURCH AND THE MARKET he calls Rothbard *one of the great economists of the twentieth century.*[40] But it is scarcely logical for a near-anarchist to sympathize with Augustine's view of the state, since Augustine sees the state as being necessary to curb man's misbehavior. Anarchists, by contrast, think it is unnecessary. Even if one assumes that there would have been no government in man's state of innocence, it cannot logically follow that there should be none in our fallen condition.

Like Novak, Woods disagrees radically with the social teachings of the Popes from Leo XIII onwards. For example, he complains that:

Rerum Novarum enshrines the critical and fateful idea that the wage rates established by market processes could be held up to moral critique by outside observers on the basis of their inadequacy in meeting the workers' material needs.[41]

How shocking! Churchmen, unversed in the academic arguments of Professor Menger, have the temerity to suggest that the market could be wrong!

Although he claims to be *a Catholic of orthodox belief,*[42] Woods clearly believes that the Popes, from Leo XIII onward, have erred in their *hostility towards the market.* He argues that they have gone

---

[39] Thomas E Woods, Jr., THE CHURCH CONFRONTS MODERNITY (New York: Columbia University Press, 2004), 125.
[40] Woods, THE CHURCH AND THE MARKET, ix.
[41] Ibid., 54.
[42] Ibid., 2.

beyond their remit in pronouncing on economic matters, on which, he argues, they are unqualified to make judgments.

This argument is mistaken. It is obvious that economics deals with important facets of human behavior. If our behavior in economic matters goes against Church teaching, the Church is surely entitled to criticize us. And while Popes are unlikely to be experts on economics, they have access to advice from experts.

Reverting to the topic of employment, we note that Woods persists in following Mises' belief that labor is chronically scarce:

> *Labor is indeed scarce relative to nature-given factors; if this were not so, there would be no unused submarginal land. If labor were ... abundant in relation to land, all land would be brought into use.*[43]

But land is only one of the non-human resources; there are also energy, minerals, timber, pure water ... In any case, if we developed all available land we would eliminate, for example, the remaining rain-forests, with grave consequences for the environment.

Many scientists believe that human consumption of the various natural resources has already reached or exceeded sustainable levels, which means that we need to refrain from further increasing our overall consumption of 'nature-given factors'.

We have thus reached the position mentioned by Mises, where labor is relatively abundant and the free labor market is, as Mises himself admits, no longer viable. Woods touches on the subject of child labor in developing countries. By no means should governments attempt to prevent this, he argues, since

---

[43] Ibid., 70.

> *If the law prevents children from being employed legally, then ... parents are likely to employ their children illegally, where conditions are almost certain to be far worse.*[44]

This is a strange remark from a man who explicitly denies that legislation can make life better for workers.[45] If it cannot, then why should conditions be worse in illegal employment? Like Novak, Woods promotes the familiar neoconservative argument that the only way to achieve better wages for the workers is to increase overall production.

The possibility of a fairer distribution of incomes is ruled out. *The more output the economy is capable of producing, the greater purchasing power will a worker's wage command.*[46] American experience over the past few decades has negated this theory; despite considerable growth, many people have seen little or no improvement in the purchasing power of their earnings; and almost all have seen their earnings grow less stable and reliable. The problem is that the rewards of growth have gone mainly to owners of capital and to overpaid top management.

On the question of labor unions, Woods quotes from Rothbard:

> *The crucial point is that unions insist on a minimum wage higher than what would be achieved for the given labor factor without the union. By doing so ... they necessarily cut the number of men (sic) whom the employer can hire.*[47]

---

[44] Ibid., 66. The phrase 'employ their children' presumably means 'find them employment'.

[45] Ibid., 63 – 73.

[46] Ibid., 59.

[47] Ibid., 74, quoted from Rothbard, MAN, ECONOMY AND STATE (1962) (Auburn, Alabama: Ludwig von Mises Institute), 623.

This conclusion, says Woods, *cannot be escaped*. But it is a grossly over-simplified view of how a business functions. Consider a company with the following data:

Sales revenue	A
Non-labor costs	B
Profits	C
Amount available for payment of wages	**D = A – B – C**

Woods says, in effect, that A, B and C are fixed quantities, so D likewise is fixed; higher rates of pay necessarily mean that fewer workers can be employed. However, in reality A, B and C are not fixed. On the contrary:

A (sales) may be too low because, for example:
- Quality is low (a better-paid workforce might achieve better quality)
- Anarchic competition (a price war) has depressed prices
- Marketing strategy is ineffective
- Products are obsolete

B (non-labor costs) may be too high because, for example:
- Production and distribution methods are wasteful
- Advertising costs and third-party commissions are too high
- Top executives are overpaid and/or enjoy excessive perquisites

C (profits) may be too high because, for example:
- Management, holding shares and options, demands excessive returns
- Outside shareholders demand excessive returns;
- The company is over-borrowed, and obliged to earn inflated profits in order to pay off its debts.

Thus, the amount a company can afford to pay in wages depends on a wide range of variables. One cannot simply assume (except, perhaps, on a very short-term view) that it is impossible to enhance wages without cutting back employment.

Woods' views on monetary policy are somewhat eccentric. He claims that

> The Federal Reserve ... is in every sense a legally privileged counterfeiter and a monopolistic one at that ... The Federal Reserve is itself the source of the erosion in the value of the dollar. That is why Austrian economists favor both a gold standard and the complete abolition of the Federal Reserve system. It is also why so many Austrians favor a 100% reserve banking system, in which banks would be legally required to back all demand deposits dollar for dollar with specie in their vaults. [48]

He even believes that this system would abolish the business cycle:

> This system alone is free from all forms of fraud, requires no violent confiscation, prevents the business cycle and avoids the 'immoral distribution effects and erosion of accumulated wealth' [inverted commas added; this periphrasis means 'inflation'] that inevitably accompany a system of fiat money. [49]

However, history tells a different story:

> Under the Gold Standard, Britain experienced very strong cyclical swings. The hundred years after resumption [of the gold standard in 1819] were marked by commercial and financial crises which recurred about every ten years ... the regularity of crises gave rise to much ... theorizing, and the Gold Standard was often cited as one of the culprits. [50]

---

[48] Ibid., 93.
[49] Ibid., 122.
[50] Prof. Marcello de Cecco (Università di Roma La Sapienza), "Gold Standard," NEW PALGRAVE DICTIONARY OF ECONOMICS, VOL. II (London: Macmillan, 1987), 541.

Historically, reliance on a gold standard has sometimes, notably during the depression of the 1930s, had severe negative consequences; the quantity of money needed to finance business has been unduly restricted by limits on the supply of gold physically available to banks.[51] Contrariwise, an upsurge in gold supplies can be inflationary, as notoriously happened in Spain in the sixteenth century, when large quantities of South American gold were imported. All this goes to show that there are no foolproof universal remedies for our economic problems; not even gold fills the bill.

IS THE GAP BRIDGEABLE?

Attempts to reconcile libertarian economics with Catholic teaching are unconvincing. For the gulf between Catholicism and libertarianism is broad and deep. One stresses the social nature of human beings, to whose lives community is essential; the other cares only about individual independence and self-sufficiency. One teaches the vital importance of good politics in building a just society; the other despises government and rejects the very notion of social justice. One calls for regulation of interpersonal contracts in the interests of justice; the other insists that everyone must be free to strike whatever bargain she chooses with anyone else. One proposes a vision of life together in virtuous society, to which we may all aspire; the other reduces all aspiration to personal ambition.

---

[51] See, for example, Brad Delong *(University of California at Berkeley)*, "Why not the Gold Standard?" at: *www.j-bradford-delong.net/Politics/whynotthegoldstandard.html* (accessed 1 July 2010).

Catholics need to recognize that libertarianism is a radically faulty doctrine because it grossly overemphasizes the autonomy of the individual, while neglecting, sometimes with contempt, the vital importance of community.

1 2

IS LIBERTARIANISM
A HERESY?

---

*Only a radical break with the dominance of the state over society could
truly satisfy the libertarians. Breaking with social justice and state inter-
ventionism would mean more than reform; it would mean admitting that
the market dominates over democracy, that individual liberty takes absolute precedence over social needs.*
VINCENT VALENTIN[1]

*Markets have become hugely efficient at responding to individual desires
for better deals, but are quite bad at responding to goals
we would like to achieve together.*
ROBERT B. REICH[2]

W hat, in a nutshell, are the fundamental errors in the doctrine and practice of economic libertarianism, and do
they justify calling it, in Catholic terms, a 'heresy'?

These errors are best seen as a complex of inter-related ideas,
many of which are not necessarily bad in themselves, but are dis-
torted or out of due proportion. We might compare these ideas

---

[1] Vincent Valentin, LES CONCEPTIONS NEO-LIBERALES DU DROIT (Paris : Economica,
2002), 369. The author is Lecturer in Law at Université Paris I.
[2] Robert B Reich, SUPERCAPITALISM (New York: Knopf, 2007), 126. The author, US
Secretary of Labor from 1993 to 1997, is currently Professor of Public Policy at University of California, Berkeley.

with the hormones[3] in the human body, each of which is necessary, but any one of which can cause serious illness if it is either deficient or present in excess. The health of the body requires correct hormonal balance. Likewise, the health of an economy and society requires fair and reasonable balances between, for example, the interests of the individual and those of the community; between the needs of workers, of consumers and of investors; between freedom of enterprise and regulation to prevent excesses and abuses.

Libertarian economic thought shows deplorably little concern with this need for balance. Too often it calls for utmost freedom for the entrepreneur, best possible value for the consumer, maximum return for the investor, keenest possible competition, minimum public spending, and other such superlatives. It is unwilling to recognize that maximizing (or minimizing) one variable generally means shrinking (or inflating) one or more other variables, often with unhappy results.

EXAGGERATED INDIVIDUALISM

Central to the libertarian complex of ideas is the exaggeration of individualism, the belief that the aspirations of the individual should take absolute precedence over the needs of the community. Some libertarians come close to rejecting the entire notion of community, as for example Adrian Wooldridge, of the British free-market journal THE ECONOMIST, who sneered that:

---

[3] See my essay "The Hyperthyroid Economy" in JOURNAL OF THE ROYAL SOCIETY OF MEDICINE (London, June 1995); *also on www.equilibrium-economicum.net* (accessed 24 July 2010)

Communities offer comfort only to people who are willing to stifle their wills and obey someone else's rules. There is no such thing as a free community. [4]

The cult of excessive individualism implies that every individual should be independent or 'self-sufficient', rejecting the notions of interdependence and solidarity. This is a totally unrealistic conception of how human society normally, and quite rightly, functions. In reality, we all depend upon the support and cooperation of others; to see this as a mark of weakness is simply perverse.

Yet the idea that near-total self-reliance is possible and desirable is a common American obsession. Some 'self-made men' have been known to totally disinherit their own children, arguing that they must make their own way, as did their fathers, without any inherited advantages. Unlike the practical Warren Buffett, who plans to leave his children enough money to do what they want to do, but not enough to allow them to do nothing!

In France, where we believe in *solidarité*, the law makes it obligatory to leave at least part of one's estate to one's children, and this is also the case generally in the Latin countries of the Americas.

MISCONCEPTION OF FREEDOM

Along with extreme individualism goes a false conception of freedom which differs radically from that found in classical Western philosophy and in the Judaeo-Christian tradition.

In the older conception, freedom is basically a positive quality which is achieved through the pursuit of goodness, justice, holi-

---

[4] Adrian Wooldridge, MERITOCRACY AND THE 'CLASSLESS SOCIETY' (London: Social Market Foundation, 1995), 18.

ness; through respect for sound laws that contribute to the common good. As Aristotle observes, *constitutional rule is a government of freemen and equals,*[5] and elsewhere,

> *He who first founded the state was the greatest of benefactors. For man, when perfected, is the best of animals, but when separated from law and justice, he is the worst of all.*[6]

The New Testament speaks of the *slavery of sin* and describes pardon as *redemption* (buying a slave out of bondage); this idea appears also in the Old Testament: *for with the Lord there is mercy, and with him is plenteous redemption. And He shall redeem Israel from all his iniquities.*[7] Thus freedom is seen as the opposite of sin, and this understanding of freedom is emphatically stated in the Catechism: *there is no true freedom except in the service of what is good and just.*[8]

By contrast, in modern libertarian thought, freedom loses contact with justice and moral goodness. It becomes simply a negative quality, namely (according to Hayek) *absence of constraints imposed by other people,* though not of constraints imposed by impersonal factors such as the free market. The pursuit of negative freedom aims to maximize the individual's scope to pursue his own inclinations, regardless of whether or not the consequences are good for the community.

This disconnection of freedom from morality leads to the notion that one cannot be free to do what is right, unless one is also free to do what is wrong. But, as we have seen, freedom should be

---

[5] Aristotle, POLITICS, Book I, 9.
[6] Ibid., 4.
[7] Psalm 130: 7, 8 (KJV).
[8] CATECHISM OF THE CATHOLIC CHURCH, Par. 1733.

understood as the opposite of wrongdoing. As one becomes, through good habit, disposition and discipline, increasingly disinclined or even unable to sin, one becomes more free. Therefore, rules against misbehavior, provided they do not prevent good behavior, do not infringe our freedom; on the contrary, they help us to be freer.

Libertarians are, quite logically in their terms, opposed to such rules. To 'set us free', they want to take away the constraints that keep us on the rails. There lies the basis for the financial deregulation that has allowed greedy, reckless, over-competitive bankers to ruin their banks and their customers, and even to gravely damage the whole world economy.

ABHORRENCE OF THE STATE

The belief that freedom means simply absence of constraint naturally implies a negative attitude to authority, whose role is largely to impose necessary constraints. With some libertarians, this negative attitude approaches or reaches anarchism; it is deeply perverse, because it diverts attention from the essential task of creating and maintaining good systems of government.

The more extreme libertarians assume that government is *ipso facto* bad, so there is no point in trying to establish good government; the only way forward is to minimize or even abolish the state. By contrast, papal teaching strongly emphasizes the vital role of the state in building a just society. And experience shows that societies in which the state is weak and ineffective are usually riddled with turbulence, corruption and injustice.

Moreover, libertarians in their abhorrence of the state call for a mini-skirt rather than a crinoline public sector. This means inadequate public services and the rejection of redistributive taxes. It is argued that the relief of poverty should be purely a matter for voluntary private charity, despite the fact that in practice that alone has never proved to be adequate.

MARKET IDOLATRY

The libertarians' argument against redistribution also reflects their explicit denial that the inequalities that arise in a free-market system are unjust. This view reflects in turn a key libertarian dogma, the belief that the market always knows best, and thus that we should never try to negate its consequences. Here we have the *idolatry of the market* condemned by John Paul II.[9]

The view that 'the market knows best' is based on the notion of 'distributed intelligence': the plethora of information on supply and demand that is diffused throughout the economy and cannot feasibly be concentrated in any planning center. Because all this information is available to 'the market', while much of it is unavailable to planners, it is held that the market is far superior to any kind of central planning.

Though this argument appears convincing in itself, against it is the reality of *market failure*, the fact that the logic of the market often leads to perverse behavior. For example, so long as hydrocarbon fuels are the cheapest available, market forces induce or compel us to go on using them, even though they are wrecking our climate.

---

[9] Pope John Paul II, encyclical CENTESIMUS ANNUS, Par. 40.

REJECTION OF THE COMMON GOOD

The theory of distributed intelligence helps to explain why libertarians by and large reject the notion, central to Catholic social teaching, of the *common good*. They argue that since politicians and planners are short of this intelligence, their ability to define what is best for the community is very limited. Moreover, pressure on individuals to act in favor of any defined common good would infringe individual freedom.

In libertarian thinking, the common good is reduced to the sum of individual goods, and achieved through the free actions of individuals in the market. But here we can very easily run into the fallacy of composition.

UNLIMITED FREEDOM OF CONTRACT

Libertarians argue that, since human beings are held to be born free and equal, therefore any individual is entitled to enter into any mutually-agreed contract with any other; any interference with this liberty is unacceptable. This idea dates back to the Enlightenment of the eighteenth century, when there were few incorporated businesses; most employers were then individual owners of small firms.

Today, of course, employers are very often large corporate legal personae rather than individuals, but libertarians hold to the late eighteenth-century view of labor relations.

This means that regulation of contracts of employment, whether by the state or by labor unions, is frowned upon.

This view was wrong even when most employers were individuals, and is even more absurd today. For parties to an employment contract are generally of unequal strength; hence, in the absence of regulation, such contracts tend to be inequitable, even though they are 'freely agreed'.

Catholic social teaching explicitly rejects the libertarian doctrine of unlimited freedom of contract in employment: *Agreement between the parties is not sufficient to justify morally the amount to be received in wages.*[10]

LABOR AS A DISUTILITY AND A COMMODITY

Libertarians hold a deplorably narrow view of the significance of work. Mises, for example, ridiculed the notion that work can be a source of human satisfaction; for him, it is nothing but a *disutility*, we do it only under pressure of necessity. It has no purpose except to generate goods or services that consumers want to buy. Therefore, no unemployment or sickness benefits! If these are available, the workers will not work.

Libertarian economic policy is narrowly focused on furthering consumer interests; it cares little, if at all, about worker interests. The economy is held to exist solely to satisfy the needs and desires of us as consumers, and in no way those of us as workers. We workers are considered to be mere instruments at the service of us consumers, precisely as John Paul II complains: *there is…a reversal of the order laid down…by the Book of Genesis: man is treated as an instrument of production.*[11]

---

[10] CATECHISM OF THE CATHOLIC CHURCH, Par. 2434.
[11] Pope John Paul II, encyclical LABOREM EXERCENS (1981), Par. 7.

Labor is regarded as no different from any other commodity; and the Austrian theory of marginal (subjective) valuation tells us that the free-market price of a commodity is the marginal price, i.e., that which the cheapest buyer is willing to pay. It follows that a free labor market has in principle no minimum wage level, not even the level of basic subsistence.

UNRESTRAINED COMPETITION AND CONSUMPTION

In the service of consumer interests, libertarians demand unrestrained competition, since this logically encourages maximum production and consumption at minimum prices. However, given that the human race as a whole appears now to be consuming natural resources at an unsustainable pace, it cannot be reasonable to encourage the richer countries to increase their consumption still further.

Moreover, excessive competition makes for deteriorating conditions of employment, precarious livelihoods, excessive risk-taking, unhealthy stresses.

Fierce competition between investment managers leads to a pathological form of capitalism that demands exorbitant returns on capital.

INEQUALITY NEVER UNJUST

Though historical and current experience shows that free markets tend to generate glaring inequalities, Austrian economic doctrine shows little or no concern over this problem. It even denies the existence of any such problem, declaring that market outcomes are inherently neither just nor unjust.

Hence inequalities resulting from the interactions of contrasting personalities in free markets cannot be called unjust. According to the Austrians, attempts by government to mitigate these inequalities are both unwarranted, since the inequalities are not unjust; and objectionable, since they obstruct the 'freedom' of market participants.

Should inequalities be so great that those at the bottom of the income scale suffer severe distress, then it falls – so Austrians argue – to voluntary charity to relieve them. Intervention by the state is admissible only as a last resort.

This theory is clearly at variance with Catholic principles, which include the doctrine of 'universal destination of goods': *each person must have access to the level of well-being necessary for his full development.*[12] Attainment of this end is a matter of justice, rather than of charity; it calls for political and legislative action:

If it is true that everyone is born with the right to use the goods of the earth, it is likewise true that, in order to ensure that this right is exercised in an equitable and orderly fashion, regulated interventions are necessary, interventions that are the result of national and international agreements, and a juridical order that adjudicates and specifies the exercise of this right.[13]

This certainly does not mean that there is no role for voluntary private charity. But it means that the construction of a just econom-

---

[12] COMPENDIUM OF THE SOCIAL DOCTRINE OF THE CHURCH, Par. 172.
[13] Ibid., Par. 173

ic framework that makes possible for all an adequate basic livelihood is a political task, as Benedict XVI reminds us:

> *Every Christian is called to practice this charity, in a manner corresponding to his vocation and according to the degree of influence he wields in the pólis. This is the institutional path – we might also call it the political path – of charity, no less excellent and effective than the kind of charity which encounters the neighbor directly, outside the institutional mediation of the pólis.* [14]

THEORY RATHER THAN PRACTICE

Finally, we mention one notably unhelpful feature of the Austrian school of libertarian economics. The Austrians, in contrast to their former antagonists, the German Historicists, greatly prefer deduction to induction. They hold that the science of economics should be based on reasoning from *a priori* assumptions about human behavior; not on the study of economic history, i.e., on observation of how economies actually function in practice.

But the assumptions adopted by Austrian economists, though allegedly axiomatic, are not necessarily realistic. They include the theory that economic behavior follows fixed laws that are the same at all times and in all places; this encourages a well-known tendency of international economic advisers, who have often tried to impose a single economic model throughout the world, regardless of local cultural and social conditions.

Another assumption is that individuals always act rationally in their own best interests: a theory which is somewhat hard to

---

[14] Pope Benedict XVI, encyclical CARITAS IN VERITATE (2009), Par. 7.

accept. One may indeed wonder whether individuals are always aware of what is in their own best interests.

HERETICAL ECONOMICS?

It is time to consider the question which the title of this chapter asks. Is economic libertarianism a heresy in the Catholic understanding of that word?

In strict theological and juridical terms, heresy is *obstinate denial ... of some truth which is to be believed by divine and Catholic faith,*[15] i.e., a truth that is held to be the word of God because it is present in the canonical scriptures, or in the Church's traditions, or in definitively proposed doctrine.

In view of the very serious disagreements we have described between libertarian economics and Catholic teachings, and of the economists' 'obstinate denial' of Catholic views on economics, it seems that a good case could be made for condemning this school of economic thought as outright heresy.

Some Catholics may disagree. But even they must surely have some difficulty in denying that libertarian economics is a *sententia haeresi proxima,* an 'opinion close to heresy'.

Such opinions have been defined as contradictions of doctrine which, though clearly Catholic, *has not been expressly 'defined' or is not clearly proposed as an article of faith in the ordinary, authorized teaching of the Church.*[16]

---

[15] CODE OF CANON LAW (Città del Vaticano: Libreria Editrice Vaticana), Canon 751
[16] Joseph Wilhelm SJ, "Heresy", THE CATHOLIC ENCYCLOPEDIA (New York: Appleton, 1907 – 1912)

SEARCH FOR A NEW EQUILIBRIUM

Libertarian economics is based on exaggeration and perversion of the pursuit of individualist values.

It first appeared in the late eighteenth century, accompanying the French Revolution; an age of breakdown of traditional authority and custom, of emerging libertarian sentiments, of rebellion against the constraints of old social orders. It has reappeared in tandem with another phase of revolt against convention, the nineteen-sixties, and has been reinforced by the collapse of its most complete antithesis, namely communism. We have overreacted against communitarianism and collectivism; and thus our culture has become too egocentric, as has happened before.

Now it is time to recognize our errors in this direction; time to strive for a new balance between our need for individual self-fulfillment and our need for the support and nurture of community; time to acknowledge our need to lead the good life together as well as on our own.

We need also to acknowledge another basic misconception. This is the notion that we can avoid the risk of tyranny by disempowering the state and handing over most of its prerogatives to the unhampered market. For the state is not the only potential tyrant. Deregulated finance can become in itself a tyrant, dominating and perverting our lives.

The current crisis is an acute modern case of an age-old problem. The power and velocity of our highly-developed markets means that, more readily than ever before, they can become our brutal, overbearing masters rather than our good servants. For a memorable expression of this timeless truth, let us turn to the Roman poet Horace, brilliantly translated in the mid-nineteenth century by the Oxford classicist John Conington:

> *Gold will be slave or master; 'tis more fit*
> *That it be led by us, than we by it.* 17

---

17 Horace, EPISTLES, Book I, no. 10, trans. John Conington (1869); see *www.gutenberg.com/etext/5419*. I quote Conington's translation because it is especially euphonious and memorable, but it is not the most accurate. Horace does not mention 'gold' but instead *collecta pecunia*, that is, 'accumulated money' or, as we would say, capital. Thus Horace's comment fits our present predicament remarkably well; the financial crisis of 2008 reflects the gross mishandling of huge, highly mobile, poorly supervised pools of capital.

BIBLIOGRAPHY

*Biblical citations are from the NEW JERUSALEM BIBLE,
unless otherwise mentioned. Papal encyclicals and other Vatican documents are accessible online at the Vatican website, www.vatican.va. Many
of the cited works by Austrian School economists are accessible online at
the site of the Ludwig von Mises Institute, www.mises.org, under the
heading 'Literature'.*

Aristotle. POLITICS, trans. Benjamin Jowett. London: Colonial Press, 1900.

Arrington, L.J. & Bitton, D. THE MORMON EXPERIENCE. New York: Knopf, 1979.

Augustine, Saint. ENCHIRIDION DE FIDE, SPE ET CARITATE [*Handbook on Faith, Hope and Charity*].

_____. DE CIVITATE DEI [*The City of God*].

_____. DE LIBERO ARBITRIO [*The Problem of Free Will*].

Babylonian Talmud. BABA BATHRA. See *www.comeandhear.com.*

Benedict XVI, Pope. Encyclical CARITAS IN VERITATE (2009).

_____. Encyclical DEUS CARITAS EST (2006).

_____. INTRODUCTION TO CHRISTIANITY [*Einführung in dasChristentum, 1968*], trans. J.R. Foster. San Francisco: Ignatius Press, 1990.

Berlin, Isaiah. FOUR ESSAYS ON LIBERTY. Oxford: University Press, 1969.

Böhm-Bawerk, Eugen von. CAPITAL AND INTEREST [*Kapital und Kapitalzins, 1889*], trans. G.D. Huncke & H.F. Sennholz. South Holland, Illinois: Libertarian Press, 1959.

BOOK OF COMMON PRAYER. New York: Church Hymnal Corporation and Sea-bury Press, 1977.

Campagnolo, Gilles. SEULS LES EXTREMISTES SONT COHERENTS. Lyon: ENS Edi-tions, 2006.

Castel, Robert. "Psychanalyse de la Crise." LE MONDE (Paris) 27 February 2009.

Chrysostom, St. John. HOMILIES ON THE EPISTLE TO THE ROMANS, trans. J.B. Morris. Oxford: Parker, 1861.

Condillac, Etienne Bonnot de. COMMERCE AND GOVERNMENT [*Le Commerce et le Gouvernement, 1776*], trans. Shelagh Eltis. Cheltenham, England and Northampton, Mass.: Edward Elgar, 1997.

CODE OF CANON LAW. Città del Vaticano: Libreria Editrice Vaticana.

Copleston, Frederick. HISTORY OF PHILOSOPHY, Vol. VIII. London: Burns & Oates, 1966.

Darcos, Xavier. Interview. LE MONDE (Paris), 1 June 2006.

De Cecco, Marcello. "Gold Standard." NEW PALGRAVE DICTIONARY OF ECONOMICS, VOL. II. London: Macmillan, 1987.

Delong, Brad. "Why not the Gold Standard?" See *www.j-bradford-delong.net/Politics/whynotthegoldstandard.html.*

Dimova-Cookson, Maria, and Mander, W.J. T.H. GREEN: ETHICS, METAPHYSICS AND POLITICAL ECONOMY. Oxford: Clarendon Press, 2006.

Droit, Roger-Pol. Review of Pierre Caye's book MORALE ET CHAOS. LE MONDE (Paris), 5 December 2008.

Dutra, Olivio. Comment. LE FIGARO ENTREPRISES (Paris), 7 February 2005.

Elazar, Daniel J. "Judaism and Politics." ENCYCLOPEDIA OF JUDAISM. Leyden: Brill, 2006.

Ely, Richard. "The Past and Present of Political Economy." JOHNS HOPKINS UNIVERSITY STUDIES IN HISTORY AND POLITICAL SCIENCE, Series 2, Part 3. Baltimore: Murray, 1884.

Emerson, Ralph Waldo. "Circles" (1841). EMERSON: ESSAYS AND LECTURES, ed. J Porte. New York: Literary Classics of the United States, 1983.

_____. "Self-Reliance" (1841). Ibid.

Gide, Charles and Rist, Charles. HISTOIRE DES DOCTRINES ECONOMIQUES (1909). Paris: Dalloz, 2000.

Gil, José Tomás Raga. "A New Shape for the Welfare State." PROCEEDINGS OF THE EIGHTH PLENARY SESSION (April 2002). Città del Vaticano: Pontifical Academy of Social Sciences.

Gloria-Palermo, Sandye and Giulio Palermo. "Austrian Economics and Value Judgments." REVIEW OF POLITICAL ECONOMY, Vol. 17, No. 1, January 2005. London: Routledge.

Godwin, William. POLITICAL JUSTICE (1798), facsimile ed. F.E.L. Priestly. Toronto: University Press, 1946.

Gray, John. BEYOND THE NEW RIGHT. London: Routledge, 1993.

Green, Thomas Hill. WORKS OF T.H. GREEN, ed. R.L. Nettleship. London: Longmans, 1895 – 1911.

Harewood, Earl of. See Lascelles, George.

Häring, Bernard. THE LAW OF CHRIST [*Das Gesetz Christi, 1951*], trans. E.G. Kaiser. Cork: Mercier, 1961.

Hayek, Friedrich von. "The Use of Knowledge in Society." AMERICAN ECONOMIC REVIEW, Vol. XXXV, No. 4 (September 1945). Reprinted in Hayek, INDIVIDUALISM AND ECONOMIC ORDER, 80.

_____. INDIVIDUALISM AND ECONOMIC ORDER. Chicago: University Press, 1948.

_____. LAW, LEGISLATION AND LIBERTY, Vol. I. Chicago: University Press, 1973.

_____. THE CONSTITUTION OF LIBERTY. London: Routledge & Kegan Paul, 1960.

_____. THE FATAL CONCEIT. London: Routledge, 1988.

_____. THE MIRAGE OF SOCIAL JUSTICE, Vol. II of Law, LEGISLATION AND LIBERTY. Chicago: University Press, 1976.

_____. THE ROAD TO SERFDOM. London: Routledge & Kegan Paul, 1944.

_____. UNEMPLOYMENT AND THE UNIONS. London: Institute of Economic Affairs, 1980.

Hess-Fallon, Brigitte and Simon, Anne-Marie. DROIT DU TRAVAIL. Paris: Dalloz, 2006.

Hildebrand, Bruno. DIE NATIONALÖKONOMIE DER GEGENWART UND ZUKUNFT [*The National Economy of the Present and Future*]. Frankfürt am Main: J. Rütten, 1848.

Hilferding, Rudolph. BÖHM-BAWERK'S CRITIQUE OF MARX [*Böhm-Bawerks Marxkritik, 1904*], trans. Eden & Cedar Paul. In KARL MARX AND THE CLOSE OF HIS SYSTEM, AND BÖHM-BAWERK'S CRITIQUE OF MARX. Philadelphia: Orion, 1984.

Horace, EPISTLES, trans John Conington (1869). See *www.gutenberg.com/etext/5419.*

Hughes, Edward. ELECTRICAL TECHNOLOGY, 6th edition. London: Longmans, 1987.

International Labor Office. WORLD OF WORK REPORT 2008. See *www.ilo.org/public/english/bureau/inst/download/world08.pdf.*

John Paul II, Pope. Encyclical CENTESIMUS ANNUS (1991).

_____. Encyclical LABOREM EXERCENS (1981).

John XXIII, Pope. Encyclical MATER ET MAGISTRA (1961).

Kennickell, Arthur B. A ROLLING TIDE: CHANGES IN THE DISTRIBUTION OF WEALTH ON THE US, 1989-2001. See *www.federalreserve.gov/pubs/oss/oss2/papers/concentration.2001.10.pdf*

Ketteler, Wilhelm von. Sermon given on 25 July 1869 at Offenbach am Main. See "Die Arbeiterbewegung und ihr Streben" in Ketteler, SCHRIFTEN, AUFSÄTZE UND REDEN 1867-1870. Mainz: von Hase und Koehler, 1978.

Knies, Karl. DIE POLITSCHE ÖKONOMIE. Braunschweig: Schwetschke und Sohn, 1853.

Kohler, Kaufmann. "Charity." THE JEWISH ENCYCLOPEDIA. New York: KTAV, 1901-1906.

Lascelles, George, Earl of Harewood, editor. KOBBÉ'S COMPLETE OPERA BOOK. London: The Bodley Head, 1987.

Layard, Richard. See citation by Catherine Mayer in TIME MAGAZINE, 7 April 2008.

Leo XIII, Pope. Encyclical LIBERTAS PRAESTANTISSIMUM (1888).

_____. Encyclical RERUM NOVARUM (1891).

Lieven, Anatole. "American freedom is a divisive concept." FINANCIAL TIMES (London), 7 August 2000.

Luttwak, Edward. "Why Fascism is the Wave of the Future." LONDON REVIEW OF BOOKS, 7 April 1994.

Manning, Henry (Cardinal). The Labour and Social Question (1891). In Manning, LA QUESTION OUVRIERE ET SOCIALE. Paris: Tolra, 1892.

Marx, Karl. GRUNDRISSE, trans. Martin Nicolaus. London: Penguin, 1993.

Menger, Carl. PRINCIPLES OF ECONOMICS [*Grundsätze der Volkwirtschaftslehre, 1871*], trans. J Dingwall & B F Hoselitz. New York: University Press, 1976.

Mill, John Stuart. ON LIBERTY (1869). New York: Liberal Arts Press, 1956.

Milner, Jean-Claude. Interview. LE MONDE (Paris), 5 February, 2011.

Mises, Ludwig von. HUMAN ACTION (1949), 4th edition. San Francisco: Fox & Wilkes, 1963.

_____. SOCIALISM [*Die Gemeinwirtschaft, 1922*], trans. J Kahane. New Haven: Yale University Press, 1951.

_____. THE ANTI-CAPITALISTIC MENTALITY. Grove City, Pennsylvania: Libertarian Press, 1990.

_____. THE ULTIMATE FOUNDATION OF ECONOMIC SCIENCE. New York: Van Nostrand, 1962.

Mueller, Anthony. "Bye-bye, Bismarck." See *www.mises.org/daily/1275*.

Novak, Michael. ON CULTIVATING LIBERTY. Lanham, Maryland: Rowman & Littlefield, 1999.

_____. THE SPIRIT OF DEMOCRATIC CAPITALISM. New York: American Enterprise Institute/Simon & Schuster, 1982.

_____. THIS HEMISPHERE OF LIBERTY. Washington, DC: American Enterprise Institute Press, 1990.

_____. THREE IN ONE: ESSAYS ON DEMOCRATIC CAPITALISM. Lanham, Maryland: Madison Books, 2000.

_____. THE ADVENTURE OF CATHOLIC SOCIAL DOCTRINE. See *www.thecatholicthing.org/2008/the-adventure-of-catholic-social-doctrine.html*.

Occupational Safety and Health Administration (OHSA). EXPERT FORECAST ON EMERGING PSYCHOSOCIAL RISKS. See *http://osha.europa.eu/en/publications/reports/7807118/view*.

Palermo, Giulio. "Are we all Keynesians?" HISTORY OF ECONOMIC IDEAS. Cambridge, England: University Press, 2005/1

Paul VI, Pope. Decree APOSTOLICAM ACTUOSITATEM (1965).

Piketty, Thomas. LES HAUTS REVENUS EN FRANCE AU XX SIECLE. Paris: Grasset, 2001.

Pius XI, Pope. Encyclical QUADRAGESIMO ANNO (1931).

Pohle, Joseph. "Merit." THE CATHOLIC ENCYCLOPEDIA. New York: Appleton, 1907-1912.

Pontifical Council for Justice and Peace. COMPENDIUM OF THE SOCIAL DOCTRINE OF THE CHURCH. Città del Vaticano: Libreria Editrice Vaticana, 2004.

Ratzinger, Joseph. See Benedict XVI.

Ricardo, David. PRINCIPLES OF POLITICAL ECONOMY (1817). In THE WORKS AND CORRESPONDENCE OF DAVID RICARDO, ed. P Sraffa and M.H. Dobb. Cambridge, England: University Press, 1951.

Ritchie, David George. NATURAL RIGHTS. London: Sonnenschein, 1895.

Roscher, Wilhelm. DIE GRUNDLAGEN DER NATIONALÖKONOMIE [*Principles of Political Economy*]. Stuttgart: J.C. Cotta, 1864.

Rothbard, Murray N. "The Celebrated Adam Smith". Chap. 16 in Rothbard, AN AUSTRIAN PERSPECTIVE ON THE HISTORY OF ECONOMIC THOUGHT. London: Edward Elgar, 1995.

_____. "The Mantle of Science." SCIENTISM AND VALUE, ed. Helmut Schoeck and James Wiggins. Princeton, New Jersey: Van Nostrand, 1960.

_____. Interview in THE NEW BANNER, 25 February 1972. See *www.mises.org/web/2667*.

_____. LUDWIG VON MISES: SCHOLAR, CREATOR, HERO. Auburn, Alabama: Ludwig von Mises Institute, 1988.

_____. MAN, ECONOMY AND STATE (1962). Auburn, Alabama: Ludwig von Mises Institute.

_____. THE ETHICS OF LIBERTY (1982). New York: University Press, 1998.

Ryan, John A. "Individualism." THE CATHOLIC ENCYCLOPEDIA, Vol. VII. New York: Appleton, 1910.

_____. A LIVING WAGE. New York: Macmillan, 1906.

Sacks, Jonathan. THE POLITICS OF HOPE. London: Vintage (Random House), 2000.

Salin, Pascal. "Il faut sauver le soldat Bolkestein!" LE FIGARO (Paris), 2 February 2005.

Schmoller, Gustav. GRUNDRISS DER ALLGEMEINEN VOLKSWIRTSCHAFTSLEHRE [*Principles of General Economics*]. Leipzig: Duncker & Humblot, 1900/04.

Scott, Sir Walter. TALES OF A GRANDFATHER (1828). Glasgow: Gowans & Gray, 1928.

Shionoya, Yuichi. THE SOUL OF THE GERMAN HISTORICAL SCHOOL. New York: Springer, 2005.

Sibley, Angus. "From Calf to Market." THE MONTH (London), August 1998, also on *www.equilibrium-economicum.net*.

_____. "The Hyperthyroid Economy". JOURNAL OF THE ROYAL SOCIETY OF MEDICINE (London), June 1995, also on *www.equilibrium-economicum.net.*

Sirico, Robert. "Mandated Giving doesn't come from the heart." RELIGION AND LIBERTY, Vol. 17, no. 4 (fall 2007). Grand Rapids, Michigan: Acton Institute.

_____. "Minimum Wage, Maximum Suffering" (15 August 2007). See *www.acton.org/commentary/commentary397.php.*

Smith, Adam. HISTORY OF ASTRONOMY. In Smith, ESSAYS ON PHILOSOPHICAL SUBJECTS, ed. W P D Wightman and J C Bryce. Oxford: Clarendon Press, 1980.

_____. THE THEORY OF MORAL SENTIMENTS (1759), ed. D. D. Raphael and A. L. Macfie. Oxford: Clarendon Press, 1976.

Thomas à Kempis. De Imitatione Christi.

Thomas Aquinas, Saint. SUMMA THEOLOGICA.

Thoreau, Henry David. WALDEN (1854). THOREAU: A WEEK ON CONCORD, ETC., ed. R F Sayre. New York: Literary Classics of the United States, 1985.

Tocqueville, Alexis de. DEMOCRACY IN AMERICA [*La Démocratie en Amérique, 1835*], trans. Henry Reeve (1839). New York: Knopf, 1945.

Turgot, Anne-Robert-Jacques. "Réflexions sur la Formation et la Distribution des Richesses" (1769), trans. P D Groenewegen. THE ECONOMICS OF A. R. J. TURGOT. The Hague: Nijhoff, 1977.

US Census Bureau (HHES). HISTORICAL INCOME TABLES (2001).

Valentin, Vincent. LES CONCEPTIONS NEO-LIBERALES DU DROIT. Paris: Economica, 2002.

Vatican Council II. DIGNITATIS HUMANAE, Declaration on Religious Freedom (1965).

_____. GAUDIUM ET SPES, Pastoral Constitution of the Church in the Contemporary World (1965).

Veryser, Harry C. "Murray Rothbard in memoriam." THE INTERCOLLEGIATE REVIEW (Wilmington, Delaware), Fall 1995.

Walras, Léon. ELEMENTS D'ÉCONOMIE POLITIQUE PURE (1874-1877), fourth edition, 1900. Paris: Pichon, 1952.

Walsh, Moira M. "Aristotle's Conception of Freedom." JOURNAL OF THE HISTORY OF PHILOSOPHY, October 1997.

Weill, Nicolas. "Althusser revient?" LE MONDE (Paris), 30 July 2008.

Whately, Richard. INTRODUCTORY LECTURES ON POLITICAL ECONOMY (1831). See *www.econlib.org/library/Whately/whtPE9.html.*

Whitman, Walt. LEAVES OF GRASS (1855). WALT WHITMAN: COMPLETE POETRY AND COLLECTED PROSE, ed. J Kaplan. New York: Literary Classics of the United States, 1982.

Wieser, Friedrich von. SOCIAL ECONOMICS [*Theorie der gesellschaftlichen Wirtschaft, 1914*], trans. A.F. Hinrichs. New York: A.M. Kelley, 1967.

_____. URSPRUNG UND HAUPTGESETZE DES WIRTSCHAFTLICHEN WERTES [*Original Source and Basic Laws of Economic Value*]. Vienna, Hölder, 1884.

Wilhelm, Joseph. "Heresy." THE CATHOLIC ENCYCLOPEDIA. New York: Appleton, 1907-1912.

Woods, Thomas E, Jr. THE CHURCH AND THE MARKET. Lanham, Maryland: Lexington, 2005.

_____. THE CHURCH CONFRONTS MODERNITY. New York: Columbia University Press, 2004.

Wooldridge, Adrian. MERITOCRACY AND THE 'CLASSLESS SOCIETY.' London: Social Market Foundation, 1995.

Yamawaki, Naoshi (editor). "Walter Eucken and Wilhelm Röpke." THE GERMAN HISTORICAL SCHOOL: THE HISTORICAL AND ETHICAL APPROACH TO ECONOMICS. Routledge: London & New York, 2001.

24574367R00141

Made in the USA
San Bernardino, CA
29 September 2015